A
TUGGING
of the
HEARTSTRINGS

A TUGGING *of the* HEARTSTRINGS

POEMS
By LAURITA MCKERCHER

To Darlene—
God's blessings
of joy & hope
from my to yours.
heart to yours.
Laurita McKercher

A SPIRITUAL JOURNEY

Pleasant Word
PW — A Division of WinePress Group

Pleasant Word (a division of WinePress Publishing, PO Box 428, Enumclaw, WA 98022) functions only as book publisher. As such, the ultimate design, content, editorial accuracy, and views expressed or implied in this work are those of the author.

Unless otherwise noted, all Scriptures are taken from the *Holy Bible, New International Version®*, NIV®. Copyright © 1973, 1978, 1984 by the International Bible Society. Used by permission of Zondervan. All rights reserved.

ISBN 13: 978-1-4141-1264-0
ISBN 10: 1-4141-1264-5
Library of Congress Catalog Card Number: 2008906149

CONTENTS

A Heart to Serve Him

A Heart to Pray

A Heart Set Free

Life Lessons for the Heart

A Heart of Gratitude

A Heart for the Holidays

Poetry is a window to the heart and soul of the poet. Such is the case with this book. Inside you will find some of the deepest thoughts, prayers, and lessons taught to me by the Creator. My prayer for you is not that you would be passively inspired, but that your heart would be changed and you would be challenged to grasp the wide scope of God's involvement in your life as you delve deep within your own soul for answers to life's perplexities. As you read and feel God tugging at your heart strings, I pray that you will allow yourself to be drawn closer to him.

To Chris Bollaert who first encouraged me to publish my works; to my wonderful husband, Scott, who made me do it; and to my beautiful girls, Jayme, Robyn, and Alexi, who made me believe it was worth it and taught me many of the lessons within. I thank God for each one of you.

A Tugging of the Heart Strings

Quiet your soul and listen
To the whisperings deep within.
Feel the tugging of your heart strings.
Let your spiritual journey begin.
Open your heart and soul
To hear what God has to say.
Let him pull your heart strings closer
As you begin each day.
The journey is never boring
When you surrender and see
The way he molds you and makes you
Into a new creation set free.
Fight any desire to follow
The things that tear you away
From the tugging of the heart strings
That bring you to God every day.

Ephesians 1:18-19a

"I pray also that the eyes of your heart may be enlightened
in order that you may know the hope to which he has called
you, the riches of his glorious inheritance in the saints, and
his incomparably great power for us who believe."

A PRAISE SONG

To God the Almighty,
Perfect and strong,
I lift up my praises
I sing you this song.
Defender, Protector,
Creator and King,
My praise to you only,
My praises I sing.
For you show your mercy
And greatness and love
To me undeserving
Of grace from above.
You call me your child
And make me your own.
Your love covers like honey
As it drips from your throne.
Goodness and mercy
For all of my days
Relieves every heartache.
For this I give praise.
To God, the Almighty,
Perfect and strong,
I lift up my praises.
I sing you this song.

Psalm 145:3

"Great is the Lord and most worthy of praise;
his greatness no one can fathom."

DAVID'S PROMISE

When God made David a promise, 'twas also made for me,
"I will build your house," he said, "And I will dwell with thee.
And when your days are over, I will offer you my rest.
You'll dwell within my presence and I will call you blessed."

Give praise to God the Father for the promises he gives.
His kingdom is forever; with him believers live.
Give praise to Jesus Christ, his Son, who came to earth and died.
He gave hope of eternal life when he was crucified.

And now he sits upon his throne close by his Father's hand,
Establishing his perfect will o'er every weary land.
That land includes your heart, you see. It also includes mine.
May Jesus live within our hearts and through us may he shine.

2 Samuel 7:11b-12

"'The Lord declares to you that the Lord himself will establish a house for you; When your days are over and you rest
with your fathers, I will raise up your offspring to succeed
you, who will come from your own body, and I will establish
his kingdom.'"

ALL NATURE SINGS HIS PRAISES

The sky is blue and nature calls to bring me back to God.
He is the gentle shepherd guiding me o'er weary sod.
I've found rest beside the waters of the gentle flowing stream.
I've seen the shining light from heaven upon the water gleam.

I've listened to the breezes blow through branches of tall pine.
I've felt the peace of nature telling me that God is mine.
I've watched the forest creatures move about without a
    care.
They have no need to worry for their God is always there.

In the stillness of the forest I can hear my Father's voice
Reminding me of him in whom I gladly will rejoice.
I revel in the knowledge that he created all of this
To still my mind and calm my heart and give me quiet bliss.

So praise to God's creation, which he gives us to enjoy.
And praise to the Creator, may my life to him employ.
And guide me, gentle Shepherd; keep me safe from all life's harms
As I nestle close and let you carry me within your arms.

Psalm 23:1-3
"The Lord is my shepherd, I shall not be in want.
    He makes me lie down in green pastures,
he leads me beside quiet waters, he restores my soul."

VICTORIOUS

The awesome, almighty, victorious King
To thee, my great Savior, my praise to you bring.
You've promised to guide me and shield me from sin
That I'd be victorious; my battles I'd win.

On eagles' wings fly me to havens of rest.
May I live victorious; die having been blessed.
May your victories ever remind me that you
Can make me victorious; my heart be renewed.

You came down from heaven to die on a tree.
And wonder of wonders, you did it for me!
Creator, Redeemer, my Savior and Lord,
In you through all ages my victories are stored.

Psalm 21:5

"Through the victories you gave, his glory is great;
    you have bestowed on him splendor and majesty."

PRAISE GOD!

Praise God! I have a perfect Lord
Who lifts me every day.
Praise God! I've found a perfect friend
Who loves me when I stray.

It doesn't matter how I feel
When things aren't going right.
I'll not forget my perfect God
Will make my future bright.

Praise God for his perspective
Of the way things ought to be.
Praise God for his great wisdom
And how he's teaching me.

Whenever things are starting to
Look grim where my feet trod,
I must stop and look above
And simply say, "Praise God!"

Psalm: 34:1

"I will extol the Lord at all times;
his praise will always be on my lips."

TO THE GOD OF EVERYTHING

To the God of all the heavens, to the God of all the earth,
To the God of every living breathing being.
To the God of all creation, to the God of you and me,
To the God who is so great our praise we sing.

To the God of every sinner, to the God of all mankind,
To the God of those who call upon his name.
To the God of things unseen here, to the God of everything,
To the God who will forever stay the same.

To the God who never falters, to the God who's ever near,
To the God who gives us mercy mixed with grace.
To the God who gives forgiveness, to the God who came to die,
To the God they crucified there in my place.

It's to this God I give, then, a living sacrifice.
It's to this God my heart is truly shown.
It is this perfect Father I trust to do what's best
For my heart is filled with love for him alone.

Jude 24-25

"To him who is able to keep you from falling and to present you before his glorious presence without fault and with great joy—to the only God our Savior be glory, majesty, power and authority, through Jesus Christ our Lord, before all ages, now and forevermore!"

THE PERFECT PAINTER

The evening sky is all aflame,
Bringing glory to his name.
For no one else paints such a scene
As this sunset so serene.
The wisps of color glowing there
Soon disappear into night air.
Such fleeting moments too soon past,
That only in our memory last.
Yet still there'll be another day,
Another chance to rise and say,
"Praise to the painter, glorious one
Who paints the sky when day is done.
Praise to Creator, Savior, Friend
Who brings us life that has no end."

Psalm 74:16

"The day is yours, and yours also the night;
    you established the sun and moon."

THE MIGHTY VICTOR

My Savior is almighty. He is the Son of God
Who came to earth to save me from my sin.
He willingly died upon a rough and rugged cross
So I might never need to die again.

The cord they used to bind him in dark Gethsemane
Could never hold the Savior very long.
The stone they used to seal him inside a darkened tomb
Could not secure God's Son, the pure and strong.

He rides with mighty splendor o'er heaven and the earth,
While all creation cries to him in need.
His righteous, holy presence resides upon his throne.
He's proven he's the Mighty One indeed.

And now he reigns forever while waiting for the day
When he can come and take his loved ones home.
He'll come in clouds of glory with shouts of victory.
That victory came when he rolled back the stone.

Matthew 26:63b-64

"The high priest said to him, 'I charge you under oath by the living God: Tell us if you are the Christ, the Son of God.'"

"'Yes, it is as you say,' Jesus replied. 'But I say to all of you: In the future you will see the Son of Man sitting at the right hand of the Mighty One and coming on the clouds of heaven.'"

ALLELUIA, HE'S VICTORIOUS!

Alleluia! Christ is risen!
Alleluia! The stone is gone!
Alleluia! He's victorious!
Power over death's been won!

Alleluia! What a Savior!
Alleluia! What a friend!
Alleluia! He's forever!
Power to bring life without end!

Alleluia! Death is conquered!
Alleluia! Fear not the grave!
Alleluia! He is mercy!
Power to heal and power to save!

Alleluia! Free forever!
Alleluia! The debt's been paid!
Alleluia! He is holy!
Power to command and be obeyed!

Alleluia! Majestic conqueror!
Alleluia! Almighty king!
Alleluia! He reigns victorious!
Lord Jesus, we your praises sing!

Psalm 45:4

"In your majesty ride forth victoriously
    in behalf of truth, humility, and righteousness;
    let your right hand display awesome deeds."

THE GOD OF ALL AGES

Praise to the God of the future.
Praise to the God of the past.
Praise to the God of creation
Whose kingdom forever will last.

To see the God of the future
I need only see days passed away
To see how his almighty hand
Was at work on this earth every day.

A day is like a thousand years
To God who times all events.
But his goodness and mercy are changeless
To those who choose to repent.

He's been my help in trials past.
He'll be there in days still ahead.
Yesterday, today and tomorrow
I know he'll do what he said.

For my God is not one of weakness
Who changes like mist in the wind.
My God is like a solid rock,
The foundation on which I begin.

Can you plant your feet in his fortress
And let him show you just where
He wants to use you and lead you?
Then let him carry you there.

Malachi 3:6a

"I the Lord do not change."

HE HAS DONE IT!

He has done it; He's alive!
God's perfect plan he did contrive.
And to completion carried out,
Never giving in to doubt.
Never setting forth in fear
And Satan's taunts refused to hear.
In perfect grace and mercy gave
Freedom from death's stony grave.
Free from pain and worry's grasp,
Simply to his hand I'll clasp;
And let him lead me ever more
To the glorious heavenly door.
To reign victorious then with him
Because he hung upon that limb.
He has done it out of love
So I could live with him above.
He has done it just for me.
He has died and set me free.
No greater love has anyone
Shown to man than what he's done.
If he did that all for me,
If he died upon that tree,
Then all my life should thus repay
Him for the life he gave that day.
May my life begin anew
To live the way he wants me to.

Psalm 22:31

"They will proclaim his righteousness
    to a people yet unborn –
        for he has done it!"

MY MIGHTY FORTRESS

I have a mighty fortress that no one ever sees.
This fortress is around me; this fortress lives in me.
God has blessed me with this gift of his protecting love.
It's all the strength I'll ever need, his pure strength is enough.
People on the outside of this fortress can't conceive
Why I've shut myself within and totally believe
That being on the inside of this fortress makes me free.
They have the misconception that prison has a hold on me.
But they are quite mistaken by what they think they know,
I am not in prison, but headed heavenward and so
I'll live with joy in sheltered care of the fortress in my heart,
Knowing that I share his strength; we'll never be apart.
Thank God for his fortress when the battles come my way.
I'll grasp on to his strength alone and cling to him each day.

Psalm 62:1-2
"My soul finds rest in God alone;
     my salvation comes from him.
He alone is my rock and my salvation;
     he is my fortress, I will never be shaken."

JOYOUS PRAISE

I love you, Lord, and I praise your name.
You give all I need and you're ever the same.
I've tried other things, people and places,
But I've found only you fill my empty spaces.
I look at the world you made in one week.
You're not hard to find for those who would seek.
I praise you because you're righteous and just.
I praise you because in you I can trust.
There's only one God, one Savior, one King,
So to you, dear Lord, my praises I bring.
And when at the end of my life on this earth
I'll die knowing you gave me my new birth.
The joy that I'll find when I'm through heaven's door
Will last me forever; there'll be joy evermore!

John 15:11

"I have told you this so that my joy may be in you and that
your joy may be complete."

OCEAN DEPTHS

God is like that mighty ocean
That's yet to be explored.
His depths are still a mystery
With hidden treasures stored.

His horizon is unending.
His power held restrained
Until the time that Christ returns;
The time that God's ordained.

The sands upon the shoreline,
Too numerous to score,
Point to those believers
Who will live forevermore.

The tides are never ceasing
Crashing on the shores of time,
As his wondrous love continues
Bringing hope and joy sublime.

May the depths of Christ restore you
As new waves upon the sea.
May his love forever bring you
To the place where you should be.

Psalm 95:3-5

"For the Lord is the great God,
    the King above all gods.
In his hand are the depths of the earth,
    and the mountain peaks belong to him.
The sea is his, for he made it,
    and his hands formed the dry land."

NO ONE GREATER

There is none from what I can tell
Who's greater than God who in heaven does dwell.
His hand is mighty; His works are great.
By his creation alone his true worth is stated.
His power and glory deserve worship and praise.
I am commanded to do this for all of my days.
Majestic is he and so lowly am I,
And without his great plan I'd be destined to die.
Who can stand boldly before his great throne?
No one at all except for his own.
His children, his created, his beloved are we;
So much that he let his Son die on a tree.
What's amazing to me is how God on high
Makes me great too, and bids me draw nigh.
I can kneel at his feet. I'm held safe in his arms.
When his Spirit's within me I'm safe from all harm.
It's because of his love I have nothing to dread.
His Son paid the price; in his steps I shall tread.
For the God who's so great gave to me who's so small
Salvation through Christ, yes, he gave me his all.

Psalm 18:35

"You give me your shield of victory,
    and your right hand sustains me;
    you stoop down to make me great."

SONG OF PRAISE

Your love reaches high to the heavens,
Your faithfulness to the skies.
My praise and worship I give you,
In your mercy I hear your reply.

Your righteousness is like mighty mountains,
Your justice is like the great deep.
I can't fathom your power and glory,
Your compassion compels me to weep.

You preserve both man and beast, O Lord,
And guard me with such tender care.
Your unfailing love is priceless.
I've searched and you're always there.

There's refuge in your wings' mighty shadow.
Your protection has never forsaken me.
I feel safe and totally guarded,
I can sleep knowing that you'll awaken me.

Your majesty and grandeur are immeasurable,
Yet you give grace and mercy so mild.
I praise you for your sovereign power,
And I'm grateful you made me your child.

Psalm 36:5-7

"Your love, O Lord, reaches to the heavens,
    your faithfulness to the skies.
Your righteousness is like the mighty mountains,
    your justice like the great deep.
O, Lord, you preserve both man and beast.
    How priceless is your unfailing love!
Both high and low among men
    find refuge in the shadow of your wings."

INFINITY

Infinite in wisdom, infinite in grace,
Infinite in mercy as I seek his holy face.
Infinite forgiveness, infinite in might,
Infinite in leading me to do the thing that's right.
Infinite in glory, infinite in love,
Infinite in healing he gives from up above.
Infinite in blessing, infinite in joy,
Infinite in building up never to destroy.
Infinite in patience, infinite in peace,
Infinite in faithfulness that gives such sweet release.
Infinite in grandeur, infinite eternal praise,
Infinite gifts he gives to last for all my days.

1 Chronicles 16:34

"Give thanks to the Lord, for he is good;
    his love endure forever."

MY GOD IS...

Awesome
Beautiful Savior
Creator
Deliverer
Endless
Faithful
Gracious
Hope
Immovable
Joy
King
Lord of Lords
Majestic
Noble
Omnipotent
Powerful
Quiet
Righteous
Shepherd
Teacher
Undeniable
Victorious
Wise
e**X**alted
Yearning
Zealous

How about your God?

Ephesians 1:3

"Praise be to the God and Father of our Lord Jesus Christ, who has blessed us in the heavenly realms with every spiritual blessing in Christ."

THE TOUCH OF JESUS

What kind of people did Jesus touch?
Who was good enough?
A little girl, a little boy,
A criminal so tough,
Widows and kings, prophets and priests,
A man with leprosy,
A homemaker, then a paralyzed man,
And men who couldn't see.
A beggar, a thief, a Samaritan girl,
And even some fishermen,
A tax collector, both rich and poor,
So many he did befriend.
The hated, the loved, he touched them all
So each one then could see
The love that he had as he walked up the hill
And died for them on Calvary.
That touch of Jesus is never kept back
Then given to just a few.
The touch of Jesus is for one and all.
My friend, it's even for you.

Matthew 14:36b
"And all who touched him were healed."

JESUS IN YOUR HEART

Is Jesus in your heart today?
Have you ever asked him in,
To make you clean and whole once more
And cleanse your heart of sin?

Is Jesus in your heart today?
Have you placed him on the throne
And let him work within your life?
Have you looked to him alone?

Is Jesus in your heart today?
If not, then wait no more.
To change your life and make it new,
Just open up the door.

Is Jesus in your heart today?
If so, then I ask why
You haven't let him have control
And gained peace by and by.

You see if he is in your heart,
Life's worries will seem small
Compared to heaven's promises
Where you will have it all.

Matthew 7:7-8

"Ask and it will be given to you; seek and you will find; knock
and the door will be opened to you. For everyone who asks
receives; he who seeks finds; and to him who knocks, the
door will be opened."

THE POWER OF CHRIST

His power engineered his escape from the grave,
For he came to this earth not to die, but to save.
And the work that began when he rose to the sky
Continues today so his people won't die.

For Christ is the one who can heal and forgive.
He is the one who allows dead hearts to live.
He gave all he had when hung on the cross.
His power is real and his work is not lost.

Are you aware of the power in you?
Do you use it each day in all that you do?
Are you challenged to live the way he desires?
Is his Spirit in you to lift and inspire?

Have you proclaimed his name to those that you meet?
Do you live life in victory or fall in defeat?
The power of Christ can live in your heart.
Please use it each day, don't let it depart.

Romans 15:18-19a

"I will not venture to speak of anything except what Christ
has accomplished through me in leading the Gentiles to
obey God by what I have said and done—by the power of
signs and miracles, through the power of the Spirit."

ATTITUDE ADJUSTMENT

An attitude adjustment is what I need today,
To seek the Lord's perfection in all I do and say.
My heart may not be in it, but obedience must come first.
My attitude adjustment must not turn from bad to worse.

If my mind leans on Jesus, my heart will follow suit.
And soon my thoughts and actions will somehow be renewed.
My life is never harder than Jesus' was to live.
Yet his attitude was perfect—and that attitude he gives.

So, Lord, help me from this day your attitude to seek.
May I learn to love all others, from powerful to meek.
May my attitude adjustment be pleasing in your sight.
May you live and breathe and work in me so I can do what's
    right.

Hebrews 12:14

"Make every effort to live in peace with all men and to be
holy; without holiness no one will see the Lord."

God's Requirements

My God doesn't require a mountain of works
To see his heavenly good.
He doesn't require a quota sheet,
Though many think he should.

He doesn't require world wide fame
To prove I have success,
Or even a list of all I've done
To prove my righteousness.

He never keeps a holy account
To put on my resume.
No earthly position need prove my worth
When others look my way.

No, my God's only desire for me
Is to constantly seek his face,
That I'll be just and merciful
And live within his grace.

For when I walk with a humble heart
And follow in his path,
His message will move to other souls
To save them from his wrath.

Micah 6:8

"He has showed you, O man, what is good.
 And what does the Lord require of you?
To act justly and to love mercy
 and to walk humbly with your God."

IN THE BEGINNING

In the beginning was the Word
And not much more to see,
But in the beginning was the Word
And all God's plans for me.

Amazing thought I find today
That through eternity
My God has known and planned my life
As it was meant to be.

How much more could he show his love
In view of what he sees?
Even though he knew I'd fail;
He lived and died for me.

Ephesians 1:11-12

"In him we were also chosen, having been predestined according to the plan of him who works out everything in conformity with the purpose of his will, in order that we, who were the first to hope in Christ, might be for the praise of his glory."

THE PATHWAY

As I walk down the path of life
I like to look around
And see the things that others miss,
The treasures to be found.

I look above through shady trees
And see sunlight moving in.
Perhaps that's like the light of God
Come to free my life from sin.

The wind blows through the leaves of trees
As in my life stirs his Spirit.
But as with the wind which so gently blows
I must learn to stop and hear it.

The well-worn path most people walk
Will lead in worldly directions.
I think I'll go the less traveled way
And search for God's affection.

The key to it all, the enjoyment of life,
Is simply to carefully choose
The pathway of life he wants me to take,
And then there's no way I can lose.

Haggai 1:5b

"Give careful thought to your ways."

THE VOICE OF THE LORD

Through raging storms and setting sun,
The voice of the Lord has just begun
To lead us to a song of grace
And give us joy in every place.

The voice of God knows yet no bounds.
He speaks and majesty abounds.
From hills and plains, from rocks and seas,
My God still stoops to speak to me.

And in his voice there's love and care.
Within his voice is joy so fair.
With power and might and glorious words,
My God demands that he be heard.

And so I listen to his voice,
And consciously I make a choice
To follow what he teaches me.
I'll love his voice eternally.

Psalms 29:3-4

"The voice of the Lord is over the waters;
    the God of glory thunders,
        the Lord thunders over the mighty waters.
The voice of the Lord is powerful;
    the voice of the Lord is majestic."

CLOUDS AND DARKNESS

The awesome mystery of God will not be clearly revealed
Until that day in heaven when eternal life is sealed.
For now, clouds and darkness are hiding our God's face.
For now, clouds and darkness keep us in this place.

To look upon the face of God would simply overpower
The human mind with human thoughts that live from hour
    to hour.
We could never fathom all the things our Father means,
And so that part of who he is, is shadowed in our dreams.

But even so he has revealed a portion every day
To those who come before his throne and take the time to pray.
Tell God, "I want to see your work throughout my daily life
In every situation that is causing grief and strife."

And God in grace and mercy will let you know he's there
Removing clouds and darkness in answer to your prayer.
And while it's true that in this life his face you may not see,
Our God in grace and mercy will respond to every plea.

Psalm 97:2

"Clouds and thick darkness surround him;
    righteousness and justice are the foundation
    of his throne."

GLORY REVEALED

The glory of the Father, manifested in his Son,
Reveals to earth God's power because the two are one.

Have you ever told yourself, "I wish I could see God"?
You can, you know, if you will look where Jesus' feet have
trod.

The glory of the Father revealed through his dear Son.
He showed us all God's attributes, then left when he was done.

And yet he sent a comforter, another in his place.
He sent the Holy Spirit so we, too, can see his face.

Now we can't understand it all; he didn't want us to.
But I know God has promised to reveal himself to you.

It's through the Holy Spirit that we can know our Lord.
It's through God's Son named Jesus that our lives can be
restored.

John 14:9b-10

"Anyone who has seen me has seen the Father. How can you
say, 'Show us the Father'? Don't you believe that I am in the
Father, and that the Father is in me? The words I say to you
are not just my own. Rather, it is the Father, living in me,
who is doing his work."

GIVEN IN LOVE

You can't give everything to Christ until you realize
How precious that you are to him; you're priceless in his eyes.
And when that knowledge comes to you and you know he
    is real,
You ask him in; his Spirit comes, and gives your heart his seal.

Complete acknowledgement of Christ and what he did for you
Will bring determination to live your life anew.
The brilliance of his presence always filling up your heart
Will shine throughout your restored soul and never will depart.

Then everything you do in life will glorify your Lord
And make you worthy of the cross where his life's blood was
    poured.
Please understand that when he died, he died for you and me.
Our lives must be lived worthy of his death that set us free.

John 10:11, 18

"I am the good shepherd. The good shepherd lays down his
life for the sheep. No one takes it from me, but I lay it down
of my own accord. I have authority to lay it down and authority to take it up again. This command I received from my
Father."

A Search For Immortality

People searching day and night for immortality
Never find the truth God gives in his reality.
They search for beauty, health, and gold, and always come
   up dry.
They search the stars and human minds to answer all their
   "whys".

It seems so meaningless to me to search in every place.
To find the purpose for your life, you ought to seek God's face.
It's in his righteousness alone that life will come to you.
It's in his word that you can find the answers that are true.

So give up chasing rainbows, eternal life to find.
It comes in giving up your will, the way I gave up mine.
God can give you answers if you only stop to ask.
Then the real immortal you will shine through the human
   mask.

Proverbs 12:28

"In the way of righteousness there is life;
   along that path is immortality."

A PARCHED HEART

Sometimes I feel that my walk with the Lord
Is covering a dry parched land.
My thirst is never wholly quenched;
My feet sinking in the sand.

I keep searching for the oasis I know
Is over the hill just beyond,
But it seems to always elude me somehow
My heart won't seem to respond.

I say all the things expected of me
To make others think I'm okay.
I talk the talk and sing the songs,
But there's a hollowness when I pray.

How did he get so far away?
And how can I bring him back?
How will I find that closeness with him
That my life just seems to lack?

Lord, I kneel down and pray that you
Will shatter the barrier here
That's blocking my communion with you
And the knowledge that you're so near.

I want my heart to swell again
The way that it used to do
When I felt your presence within my life.
Lord, help me my spirit renew.

Psalms 143:6

"I spread out my hands to you;
     my soul thirsts for you like a parched land."

LOST IN THE MASSES

I walked alone among the masses
Of people on the street.
I couldn't help but feel afraid
Of strangers I would meet.
So vulnerable it seemed I was
Out walking in the world,
Where cruelty and disregard
For other souls were hurled.
It seemed so easy to lose track
Of God and of his love,
For humans have such disregard
For wisdom from above.
They've been used by Satan's best
To conceal God and his power,
So people wander all through life
Living from hour to hour.
An insignificant being
On this earth some start to feel.
Like God could never hear us
When we look to him in appeal.
But I want you to remember
He knows more than you think.
He's numbered every hair
And he will not let you sink.
You must remember who God is
The almighty conquering King
Who created each one in his heart
With the hope his joy would bring.

So next time in the masses
When you feel completely alone,
Remember God the Father
Is still sovereign on his throne.

Matthew 10:29-31

"Are not two sparrows sold for a penny? Yet not one of them will fall to the ground apart from the will of your Father. And even the very hairs of your head are all numbered. So don't be afraid; you are worth more than many sparrows."

In His Shadow

I am just a shadow hiding in the grace of God.
I am only dust settled on this old earth's sod.
Fleeting for an instant through my earthly path,
I am just a shadow deserving of his wrath.

I am just a shadow imitating him,
A dull reflection of his presence shining very dim.
I live within his shadow going with him everywhere.
I trust him in his closeness to keep me from sin's glare.

I am but a shadow of the righteous mighty Christ.
Created in his image, for me he paid the price.
Protected in the shadow of a Savior's loving heart,
I never need feel lonely for his presence won't depart.

He reveals the things of darkness and brings them into light.
To me he gives new knowledge and gives me his insight.
There's not another being I'd be a shadow to,
Than Christ who is my Savior; I know his love is true.

Job 12:22

"He reveals the deep things of darkness
    and brings deep shadows into the light."

THE CLUTTERED MIND

Sometimes my mind is cluttered
With many earthly things,
Instead of setting thoughts on God
And all the joy he brings.

If I could only focus
On what he wants me to
Then life would be much simpler
In all I say and do.

If my heart, my mind, my life
Is hidden in his love,
I'll find the guidance that he gives
Raining from above.

So help me Lord, prioritize
And stretch my time some way,
That I will thus accomplish
Your will for me today.

Colossians 3:1-3

"Since then you have been raised with Christ, set your hearts on things above, where Christ is seated at the right hand of God. Set your minds on things above, not on earthly things. For you died, and your life is now hidden with Christ in God."

MAN OF SORROWS

God saw a tender, green shoot, sprouting tall,
Man rejected; gave him sorrow and grief.
God created the plan,
Man carried it through.

God saw relief from our sorrows and sadness.
Man chose to bruise him and wound him.
God saw in him peace,
Man lashed him in violence.

God laid on him guilt and sin of all men.
Man laid him on the cross for slaughter.
God gave him the choice,
Man forced him to make it.

God gave him new life after his anguish.
Many reject the new life he gives back.
Such is the love of God,
Such is the logic of man.

Isaiah 53:12
"Therefore, I will give him a portion among the great,
    and he will divide the spoils with the strong,
because he poured out his life unto death,
    and was numbered with the transgressors.
For he bore the sin of many,
    and made intercession for the transgressors."

THE CARPENTER'S HANDS

The carpenter's hands are rough, yet so tender.
He holds me with strength and I fully surrender
To his loving touch that will carry me though.
It's the carpenter's hands I cling to.

The carpenter's hands began work as a boy
Bringing visions of hope and visions of joy
To all that he touched with his loving embrace.
It's the carpenter's hands that bring grace.

The carpenter's hands can heal and forgive
And give each of us a new reason to live.
He gave up the glory and earthly renown,
Now the carpenter's hands hold a crown.

The carpenter's hands have been pierced by mankind,
Yet he still holds them out to any who'll find
The peace and the joy that come only from him.
They were held out once before on a limb.

It's the carpenter's hands that I run to each day,
The carpenter's hands that I reach for to pray.
The carpenter's hands I can never repay.
Thank God for the carpenter's hands.

John 3:35

"The Father loves the Son and has placed everything in his hands."

THE FROST OF LIFE

There's frost on the window this morning.
It's so cold to my touch.
And when I try to see outside
I can't see very much.

The frost completely blinds me
From what I want to see.
And when I try to wipe it off
It comes right back with glee.

It reminds me of so many things
That happen every day.
The things that blind my sight of him,
He seems so far away.

Only he can kill the frost
That threatens to divide
Me from his love and presence needed
To clearly teach and guide.

And once that he has done that
I know I will clearly see
That he is always present.
He will never run from me.

Psalm 147:16

"He spreads the snow like wool
    and scatters the frost like ashes."

A SINGLE FLAME

A single candle burning in the darkness of my room
Stands nobly on the table straining to dispel the gloom.
It's only one small candle flame, flickering to and fro,
But without its tiny light the darkness soon would grow.
How like the light of Jesus which also stands alone
Dispelling dark within me where his word's been sown.
His light replaces death with life to all who would believe
And in so doing we are blessed; new life we have received.
But even in believers' lives are times where things grow dim,
Soon it becomes an anxious task to know where to find him.
It's in those times of darkness that we must dare not give in
To fear and separation when the doubt-filled thoughts begin.
Instead remember who you are and what he does for you.
He'll dispel the dark of doubting and faithfully renew
The joy you find in living with the light he gives each day.
He is the single flame chasing the darkest gloom away.

John 1:4-5

"In him was life, and that life was the light of men, the light
shines in the darkness, but the darkness has not understood
it."

EYES OF COMPASSION

Have you seen those eyes of compassion
Looking deep into your heart?
Have you seen the love that he has there,
That he wants to give you a part?

The joy of being his loved one
Is knowing that he really cares,
And he has a heart of compassion
That he gives when no one else dares.

Those eyes full of kindness and mercy
Shine down on all who believe.
They take all your pain and your sorrow
And give comfort whenever you grieve.

But first you have to focus
On the hope and love that he gives.
Then those eyes of compassion and mercy
Can give you new life to live.

Have you heard his voice of compassion
Telling all that he wants you to know,
Of his love and joy and forgiveness,
Of peace in your heart he'll bestow?

You must look to his eyes of compassion
So that you will know your true worth
As his child who is loved and cared for;
Who through that love gained rebirth.

Lord, give me your eyes of compassion
To see others the way that you do.
That I might share your hope of redemption
Bringing joy and salvation anew.

Matthew 9:36

"When he saw the crowds, he had compassion on them, because they were harassed and helpless, like sheep without a shepherd."

FOR ME, FOR YOU

Lord, soon it will be Resurrection Day,
And I think of that tomb in which you lay.
The cold and the dark and the dampness there, too.
You lay there for me, could I do that for you?

What thoughts and what feelings did you feel this week?
You showed righteous anger and hope to the meek.
When you cleansed the temple, it was long overdue.
You cleansed it for me; will I be cleansed for you?

Then you faced those church leaders full of malice and hate.
They tried to trap you; you refused to debate.
Their hypocrisy deep, you revealed them straight through.
You stood boldly for me; can I stand boldly for you?

Then you taught your disciples and knelt down to pray,
Sweating drops of your blood in anguish that day.
The whole world's sin on the cross you'd renew.
You carried my burdens; will I give them to you?

Lord, they beat you and mocked you and spit in your face.
They stripped you and flogged you and brought you disgrace.
Yet you carried that cross; oh, it was my cross, too!
Lord, you died in my place; can I live, then, for you?

Romans 12:1

"Therefore, I urge you, brothers, in view of God's mercy, to offer your bodies as living sacrifices, holy and pleasing to God—this is your spiritual act of worship."

GOD'S WORD

Because the word of God is perfect, I will strive for perfection.
Because the word of God gives protection, I will protect it
in my life.
Because the word of God is wisdom, I will strive to be wise.
Because the word of God gives joy, I will strive to be joyous.
Because the word of God is light, I will strive to give light
to others.
Because the word of God is pure, I will strive to be pure.
Because the word of God is eternal, I will focus on the
eternal.
Because the word of God is just, I will show justice to others.
Because the word of God is more desirable than gold, I will
not place gold above it.
Because the word of God is sweeter than honey, I will spread
his word like honey.
Because the word of God warns me of harm, I will heed its
warning.
Because the word of God gives success with obedience, I will
obey none other but him.

Psalm 19:7-11

"The law of the Lord is perfect,
    reviving the soul.
The statutes of the Lord are trustworthy,
    making wise the simple.
The precepts of the Lord are right,
    giving joy to the heart.
The commands of the Lord are radiant,
    giving light to the eyes.

The fear of the Lord is pure,
 enduring forever.
The ordinances of the Lord are sure
 and altogether righteous.
They are more precious than gold,
 than much pure gold;
They are sweeter than honey,
 than honey from the comb.
By them is your servant warned;
 in keeping them there is great reward."

DROP BY DROP

Drop by drop time slips away,
God's gift of life will soon end.
Second by second it can't be replaced,
Each day he will not suspend.

Each moment so precious, too precious to lose,
Each moment cannot be replaced.
How should we use the time that we have?
Each moment's too precious to waste.

Think of the things that tug you away
That really won't last very long.
A vapor, a mist, too soon burned away,
Are they worthy of eternal song?

Are they things the angels raise to God
In praise for what you have done?
Or will they soon vanish at the day's end,
Disappear with the setting of sun?

Here is the challenge given to us
Who believe and trust in his name—
Use every drop of the time that you have
To do what his glory proclaims.

Hosea 10:12

"Sow for yourselves righteousness,
    reap the fruit of unfailing love,
and break up your unplowed ground;
    for it is time to seek the Lord,
until he comes
    and showers righteousness on you."

CONSUMED

What does it mean to be consumed,
Devoured completely by Christ;
To fill every part of my self-centered soul?
Am I willing to pay such a price?

How can my heart be totally filled
With the thoughts that only God gives?
When will my soul surrender it all
To the one perfect Savior who lives?

Will I let him consume my every thought?
Every deed that he asks me to do?
Am I ready to let holy fires start to burn
And then trust him to bring my soul through?

What is it now that I'm willing to give?
How far will I let my God go?
Consumed by his touch, will I give in to that?
Will my heart yearn to fully him know?

Lord, make today the day I let go,
To you now I give you my all.
Consume me today, make me totally yours.
Today Lord, I answer your call.

Hebrews 12:28-29

"Therefore, since we are receiving a kingdom that cannot be shaken, let us be thankful, and so worship God acceptably with reverence and awe, for our 'God is a consuming fire.'"

MY LIFE'S DESTINY

Where will you take me today, dear Lord?
What's my life's destiny?
What are the things I must say and do
To show that your heart's in me?

Tomorrow, the next day, and years after that,
I calmly commit them to you,
That you might fulfill my life's destiny
As I do what you want me to do.

Give me a servant's heart that's prepared
To stand and answer your call.
Give me the courage to risk and be bold
When you ask me to give you my all.

Help me to trust in my destiny
As you hold my life in your hands.
Help me surrender with joy and in peace
To your will and your God-given plans.

Help me remember your faithfulness
To the loved ones you claim as your own.
Help me fulfill my life's destiny
And remind me I'm never alone.

Psalms 73:16-17

"When I tried to understand all this,
    it was oppressive to me—
till I entered the sanctuary of God;
    then I understood their final destiny."

A Promise Is a Promise

You kept your end of the bargain, Lord,
And answered my every prayer.
Your way is always perfect and
I delight in all your care.

You carry me and lift me up
Whenever I am down.
And as your word has promised me
Some day I'll have a crown.

For now, I must remember that
I promised something, too.
When I last faced some troubled time
It was you who brought me through.

Because you taught me loyalty.
I'll walk as you have walked.
And maybe by the grace of God
I'll talk as you have talked.

And so today I pledge my life,
My faith and all my heart
To do what I have promised, Lord,
I'll seek to do my part.

Psalms 66:13-14

"I will come to your temple with burnt offerings
    and fulfill my vows to you—
vows my lips promised and my mouth spoke
    when I was in trouble."

Do Right

Do what is right and do what is just.
It seems that I can't, but God says I must.
For if we, his people, won't obey his commands,
Then we as his people face his reprimands.

But if we maintain and do what is right,
Then we as his people are cleansed in his sight.
He gives us deliverance; salvation revealed.
For those who do right, with his Spirit are sealed.

Our time on this earth will fly by in a flash,
But his banner of love will be worn like a sash
Across every heart who lives out that love.
So do what is right for your God up above.

Isaiah 56:1

"This is what the Lord says:

'Maintain justice
    and do what is right,
for my salvation is close at hand
    and my righteousness will soon be revealed.'"

WISDOM'S PATH

Each day I have a choice to make
Of where I want to go.
Will I choose the path of wisdom's way
And reap good things I sow?

Each day builds on another and
I know I can't look back.
The past is gone; God makes me new
And keeps me on the right track.

His wisdom is not fleeting.
It grows stronger everyday.
I'll simply ask for wisdom's path
Each time I kneel to pray.

And then I'll walk in good men's ways.
My path will be made right.
Then God will say, "Well done, my child,
You're precious in my sight."

Proverbs 2:1,9,20
"My son, if you accept my words
    and store up my commands within you,
then you will understand what is right and just
    and fair—every good path.
Thus you will walk in the ways of good men
    and keep to the paths of the righteous."

THE CHALLENGE

What have I done for Christ today
That's worthy of his call?
Have I served him as I should?
Have I given him my all?

When I stand before his throne
His judgment call to face,
What will he think of all I've done?
Is there reason for disgrace?

It's easy to go through every day
And think of self alone.
The challenge? Live as Jesus lived;
Stand worthy before his throne.

And so my prayer becomes today
To give my very best
So that I can face his challenge
And find eternal rest.

Revelation 20:13

"The sea gave up the dead that were in it, and death and Hades gave up the dead that were in them, and each person was judged according to what he had done."

GOD'S CHILD

What greater gift could God ever give
Than the right to be called his child?
He took a sinner like me into his heart
And made perfect my soul once defiled.

His motive for this is hard to perceive,
A motive not many have heard of.
He wrote down his reasons, preserved in his word,
His motive, my Father's great love.

A privilege often taken for granted,
This love from the Father on high.
To be part of his family came with a price,
For me, his Son had to die.

If I'm truly God's child, then I should walk
By following his footsteps each day.
For Jesus, my brother, died on the cross
To show me the truth and the way.

1 John 3:1a-c

"How great is the love the Father has lavished on us, that
we should be called the children of God! And that is what
we are."

WILL HE FIND FAITH?

On the day that Jesus comes, just what will he find?
A willingness of heart and soul, a unity of mind?

Will he, the Faithful, find the faith in those who do profess
To be his followers and friends, who say their sin's confessed?

Will he find us living out his teachings every day?
Or will he find us battling to live our lives our way?

What would you like for him to see as he examines you?
A faith that's held up under stress, a heart that's pure and
  true?

Dear friend, he gave his life for you—the most that he
  could give.
If he did that, then shouldn't you be faithful as you live?

Will Jesus find us faithful on the day that he returns?
He will if each believer lives the faith he's helped them learn.

Luke 18:8b
"However, when the Son of Man comes, will he find faith
on the earth?"

MY PURPOSE

My purpose on this earth is very, very, clear.
I'm to do the will of God in obedience while I'm here.
My will may not be his, so I must strive to hear
The wisdom of my God as he whispers in my ear.

Jesus knew his task was to do his Father's will,
So he worked with sweet surrender upon this earth until
They crucified his body up on top of Calvary's hill.
But that was not the end for all who listen and are filled.

For Jesus still is working his task upon the earth,
For you and me and all who come to him can have rebirth.
He came to give eternal life to all who will unearth
The mysteries of almighty God who gives us our true worth.

John 6:38

"For I have come down from heaven not to do my will but
to do the will of him who sent me."

AM I LISTENING?

How can I call you Master when I do whatever I wish?
How can I be obedient when I follow my own desires?
How can I follow you when I'm walking in the opposite
   direction?
How can I hear your voice when my ears I've closed?

Do what you will, Lord. I'm finally listening!

2 Peter 2:19b

"For a man is a slave to whatever has mastered him."

ANOTHER CHANCE

Another day, another chance
To live the way I should.
Another dream I'll carry out.
I never thought I could.

Another hope to reach for
As I seek to do God's will.
Another time to come before
The Lord and remain still.

Another choice he gives me
As I journey down life's road.
Another chance to worthy be
Of Christ's blood overflowed.

Another quest to do what's right
And live within his grace,
For I don't know the day that I
Will see my Savior's face.

Matthew 24:36

"No one knows about that day or hour, not even the angels
in heaven, nor the Son, but only the Father."

A Truth to Die For

Why should I die for truth?
Is that my Christian call?
Does Jesus Christ require me
To truly surrender all?

Why is that important?
What has God done for me?
What was the truth then proven?
What is the truth God sees?

He gave me grace and mercy
And a joyful victory.
He gave me peace and comfort.
From death's fear he set me free.

He gave me truth and wisdom
That filled my heart and soul.
He freed me from my sinfulness.
Forgiveness made me whole.

Why should I stand and die for truth?
Why should I heed his plea?
Because he loves me as I am
And chose to die for me.

Acts 4:29-30

"Now, Lord, consider their threats and enable your servants
to speak your word with great boldness. Stretch out your
hand to heal and perform miraculous signs and wonders
through the name of your holy servant Jesus."

ETERNAL THINGS

Another day you gave me
To do with as I will.
What things have I accomplished?
What soil did I till?

Each day on earth we're given
A day that's too soon passed.
What kinds of things have I done?
Are they the things that last?

Some choices so important
Of value very great
Are often pushed aside
And made instead to wait.

So may I choose eternal things
That God wants me to choose.
May I accomplish what he wants.
His reward I will not lose.

Proverbs 8:10

"Choose my instruction instead of silver,
    knowledge rather than choice gold,
for wisdom is more precious than rubies,
    and nothing you desire can compare with her."

TAKE ME TO THE CROSS

Take me to your cross today. Remind me where you've been.
Remind me of the pain you felt to free me from my sin.
Sometimes I take for granted the gift you gave to me,
Your willingness to give your life and die in agony.
Beaten, bruised, and crucified by evil wicked men,
Yet when I sin I know I hurt you time and time again.
So at the foot of your rough cross I kneel before you now
And ask for your forgiveness, Lord, to make me clean
    somehow.
May I satisfy your love so I can be made whole.
And may I live a life that's worthy of your suffering soul.

Isaiah 53:11
"After the suffering of his soul,
    he will see the light of life and be satisfied;
by his knowledge my righteous servant will justify many,
    and he will bear their iniquities."

JARS OF CLAY

I am but a jar of clay concealing God's pure treasure.
I aim to live a holy life giving God great pleasure.

His message of salvation came to me when I was weak.
I'm just a fragile jar of clay who listens when he speaks.

Even though I'm very frail he uses me to spread
His message of forgiveness, bringing life to those once dead.

It's odd that he would place such worth into this jar of clay,
But God sees me as his to use to satisfy his way.

So, Lord, please fill this jar of clay with water from your
Spirit,
And send me forth to share your word and prepare those
hearts to hear it.

2 Corinthians 4:7
"But we have this treasure in jars of clay to show that this
all-surpassing power is from God and not from us."

WHAT AM I LIKE?

What kind of seed am I?
Am I good or am I bad?
Will I produce good fruit,
Or just wish I had?

What kind of soil am I?
Rocky, thorny, good?
Does my heart accept God's word,
Or only think I should?

What kind of heart have I?
Pure and filled with him?
Is his Spirit on the throne,
Or is my situation grim?

What kind of child am I?
Adopted by the King?
Do I live in full obedience,
Or still do my own thing?

What kind of person am I?
If I truly do believe,
I am fruitful, good, and pure.
For sin has been relieved.

What kind of person are you?
Have you yielded everything
Within your heart and soul and mind
Giving joy back to the King?

Matthew 13:23

"But the one who received the seed that fell on the good soil is the man who hears the word and understands it. He produces a crop, yielding a hundred, sixty or thirty times what was sown."

A CHILD OF OBEDIENCE

I have a child of obedience
Who wants to do everything right,
And when she fails in that effort
She's miserable in her plight.

Yet she gave me the wish to be righteous,
The passion to follow my Lord.
She taught me that determination
Comes with power from God's mighty sword.

She tries awfully hard to be pleasing
In action, in word, and in deed.
Stepping with faith every moment
That Jesus will meet every need.

While both of us find we keep falling,
We know that the gift of his grace
Will bring us back to his presence
As we focus each day on his face.

Thank God for my child of obedience,
For the privilege of watching her grow
In faith as well as in stature
Till in heaven perfection she'll know.

Psalm 119:40

"How I long for your precepts!
    Preserve my life in your righteousness."

How's My Love Life?

Am I patient and kind? Not always—not enough.
Am I envious and jealous? Sometimes.
Am I selfish and rude? Too often.
Do I demand my own way? Afraid so.
Am I irritable and touchy? On too many days.
Do I hold grudges? At times.
Do I rejoice at injustice? Once in a while.
Do I love no matter the cost? Not like Jesus did.

His is the perfect love.
He gave up everything.
Why can't I do the same for him?

1 Corinthians 13:4-7

"Love is patient, love is kind. It does not envy, it does not boast, it is not proud. It is not rude, it is not self-seeking, it is not easily angered, it keeps no record of wrongs. Love does not delight in evil but rejoices with the truth. It always protects, always trusts, always hopes, always perseveres."

LIFE'S MIST

A mist hangs over the lake today
Bringing shadows that seem to adorn.
The sunrise colors it subtly.
It seems a new day has been born.

It provides an air of mystery
That quickly needs to be shed.
For as soon as the sun grows warmer
The mist will be pushed on ahead.

The moments of mist are so fleeting.
They last only moments before
The mist burns away completely,
To appear on the lake nevermore.

What is life, but a mist too soon vanished;
A blur that will soon pass away?
Protect precious moments you're given
And make priceless your use of today.

James 4:14

"Why, you do not even know what will happen tomorrow. What is your life? You are a mist that appears for a little while and then vanishes."

HE CALLED OUT MY NAME

I heard the Lord calling my name one day,
On my pillow I rested, my head softly lay.
He called and he called until I heard his voice
And knew in my life I must now make a choice.

He called out my name; I said I would go
And determined to listen to his voice and show
Him how much I love the life he has shown.
He's given me riches and treasures unknown.

His call changed my life; I'll not be the same.
Things seem so much different since the day that he came
To rebuild my thoughts, my body and soul.
His call made me different and it made me whole.

He called out my name. I said, "Lord, use me."
Now I can't believe how great life can be.
He called out my name; I'm so glad he did.
My life's been joyful since I answered his bid.

Now I call his name too, and he's always there
To come when I need him and my life repair.
He's Savior and Lord and he'll strongly defend,
Yet he's also so gentle, my very best friend.

Will you answer his call? Will your answer be yes?
Will you let him come and make you the best?
Will you answer his call? For there's no other way
To feel Christ's compassion and love every day.

1 Samuel 3:9-10

"So Eli told Samuel, 'Go and lie down, and if he calls you say, "Speak, Lord, for your servant is listening."' So Samuel went and lay down in his place.

The Lord came and stood there, calling as at the other times, 'Samuel, Samuel!' Then Samuel said, 'Speak, for your servant is listening.'"

THE TIGER

Hidden deep within the heart
A sleeping tiger hides.
Aroused when forced to take a stand,
In patience he abides.
Remaining dormant and unseen
Until the time should come
When he must stand and fight with force
The battle to be won.
No one can stop the tiger's drive
Except one thing alone,
It's only when he gives it up
And takes loss as his own.
It's sheer determination
That will bring the final win
In the battle of the tiger
That you must now begin.
Go forth and fight with confidence
In what's hidden deep inside.
You'll find the tiger's victory
On the battle's other side.

Philippians 4:13

"I can do everything through him who gives me strength."

THE WAVES OF LIGHT

Looking back I can see the times God carried me.
The times when on my strength alone I couldn't even see
What needed to be done that day or where I had to go.
It's only by his gentle touch that I could face my woe.

He picked me up each morning and sent me through the
   motions
Of moving forward in my life as waves move through the
   oceans.
The waves are guided by his hand with powerful control.
They simply go the way he sends and with the tide they roll.

And when they reach the land they stop to roll back to the sea
To become a part of ocean life the way that it should be.
I know he's done the same for me when I seem to have
   crashed.
When every hope and dream I'd known seemed so completely
   dashed.

But like the waves he picked me up and moved me into life
Where I could use my hurts and pain for others in their strife.
And when I find that what I've done and all that I have known
Can encourage others, then I find I, too, have grown.

I'll hang onto God's presence whenever life seems dim,
Because I know my only hope is found through trusting him.
As sunset shows his glory in the evening's fading light,
So may his love shine forth through me so gloriously bright.

Isaiah 63:8-9

"He said, 'Surely they are my people,
    sons who will not be false to me';
    and so he became their Savior.
In all their distress he too was distressed,
    and the angel of his presence saved them.
In his love and mercy he redeemed them;
    he lifted them up and carried them
    all the days of old."

FRAGILE LIVES

A life is sometimes fragile
With a breaking heart inside,
God sees the hurt and feels the pain.
He cries the tears you cry.

When the future seems so futile
With no hope of release,
It's God who comes to calm the heart
And give his sense of peace.

When your body is so weary
And you feel you can't go on,
It's God who comes and picks you up
And takes you to the dawn.

When your soul is crushed and broken
And fear is closing in,
Remember that your God is near
And you can trust in him.

While the rest of us may fail you
In what we do or speak,
God strengthens the weary
And gives power to the weak.

Life's full of "Whys" and "I don't knows",
The outlook often grim,
But God will give you all you need
Just turn your eyes on him.

Isaiah 40:29-31

"He gives strength to the weary
     and increases the power of the weak.
Even youths grow tired and weary,
     and young men stumble and fall;
but those who hope in the Lord
     will renew their strength.
They will soar on wings like eagles;
     they will run and not grow weary,
     they will walk and not be faint."

THE PRESENCE OF THE FATHER

Do not be discouraged, friend, for what they say is true.
No matter what you're facing now, God knows the best for
  you.
He'll hold you close within his heart and give you loving care.
He'll lift you up and let you know that he is always there.

I know sometimes it's hard to feel his presence and his touch,
But please have faith that he's nearby and loves you very much.
Don't let your feelings fool you into thinking you're alone.
No matter what comes over you, your God is on his throne.

He's working every minute in all your stress and strife
So that his work will be displayed in the living of your life.
Be strong in faith and courage as you face another day,
And know that God will be nearby each time you kneel to
  pray.

John 9:3b

"But this happened so that the work of God might be displayed
in his life."

OUR AMAZING GOD

How can a God who is so big love me who feels so small?
How could he come to earth and hang upon a tree for all?
I'll never understand his plan that included death for him,
And yet I know his way is good; his love fills to the brim.

He comes to me in quiet times when I'm laying in my bed
And fills me with his Spirit who through my being spreads.
He speaks to me in sunsets and in my children's words.
His majesty and power are there; I know because I've heard.

No one will ever love you more while you live upon this earth.
He proved that coming willingly through a virgin's holy birth.
A little, tiny, helpless babe down to this earth was hurled.
Never did the birth of anyone have such impact on the world.

I hope that you can grasp his love and hang on really tight.
The only way to peace and joy is faith in his pure might.
Let the shadows fall behind you; you have a God who cares.
And when you walk toward the light, your God will answer
  prayers.

Psalm 8:4

"What is man that you are mindful of him,
    the son of man that you care for him?"

REMEMBER

Help me remember who I am today
I am a child of the King.
No one can take his love away
Even when my poor heart stings.

Others may seek to put me down
And make me feel alone,
But the King will take away my frown
And bring me to his throne.

I am a child of the Mighty King
My worth is great in his eyes.
I'm treasured and loved more than anything
My heart he'll never despise.

So to those who hurt me so,
Who wish I'd go away,
Jesus loves me, this I know.
In him I'll forever stay.

1 John 4:4

"You, dear children, are from God and have overcome them, because the one who is in you is greater than the one who is in the world."

THE LORD LOOKS DOWN

My eyes may flow unceasingly with no hope for relief,
But God looks down from heaven and sees my every shred
of grief.
And when he does he renews my faith and strengthens my
belief.
He helps me see that sorrow's pain on earth is very brief.

For in the timing of our God, each day is but a piece
Of the puzzle called eternity where time will never cease.
Each puzzle piece that he puts in will only then decrease
The time that's left until we reach our suffering's release.

So when in times of suffering you feel like you can't stand,
And when you pray with flowing tears to leave this weary
land,
Remember that your God won't let you sink beneath the sand.
He'll hold you up and keep you safe within his sovereign
hand.

Lamentations 3:49-50

"My eyes will flow unceasingly,
    without relief,
until the Lord looks down
    from heaven and sees."

MY FATHER'S HANDS

My Father's hands have led me many places in my life.
He's guided me through troubles and led me through my strife.
There's never been a moment when I thought he wasn't there
To give me strength and courage, to show me love and care.

My Father's hands have lifted me when I could not go on,
Those times when burdens buried me and my own strength
    was gone.
I know he's given hope and joy to help me through my years.
I know it was my Father's hand that wiped so many tears.

I've felt my Father's hand upon me when I was in need.
He's never failed to come to me to guide both work and deed.
It's only through his loving touch I make it through each day.
Thank God, I know my Father's hands are in my life to stay.

Isaiah 33:2
"O Lord, be gracious to us;
    we long for you.
Be our strength every morning,
    our salvation in time of distress."

TEARS OF HEALING CONTENT

Raindrops roll gently down the windowpane
Bringing cleansing, cool relief.
Teardrops roll softly down my cheeks
Bringing healing for my grief.

Some look outside and see gray clouds
And curse the gloomy rain.
Some look at me and see my tears
And only see my pain.

You need to know there's more to grief
Than pain and endless tears.
Because in Christ there's also hope
And great release from fears.

Jesus knows what it's like to grieve.
God's word says that he wept.
When Lazarus died, he shed those tears,
But he knew God's word would be kept.

From death to life his friend was returned
After all the tears had been spent.
There's healing that comes through the knowledge of Christ;
Sweet healing of joyful content.

2 Kings 20:5a-b

"Go and tell Hezekiah, the leader of my people, 'This is what
the Lord, the God of your father David, says: I have heard
your prayer and seen your tears; I will heal you.'"

DROWNING IN THE DUST

My life seems dry. I almost feel
I'm drowning in the dust.
I can't go on. I'm tired, Lord,
And yet I know I must.

I wake up every morning
Wanting only night again,
So I can crawl back into bed.
Sleep seems my only friend.

Yet faith and logic tell me
That is simply not the case.
I have your love within my heart
In a special hidden place.

I know that you will bring me
To your well that's never dry.
You'll quench the thirst within my soul
And wipe the tears I cry.

But I must make the choice, Lord,
To drown or choose to drink.
The waters of revival's joy
Are closer than I think.

John 4:13-14

"Jesus answered, 'Everyone who drinks this water will be
thirsty again, but whoever drinks the water I give him will
never thirst. Indeed, the water I give him will become in
him a spring of water welling up to eternal life.'"

GRASP ON

Grasp on to God's almighty hand
And never let him go.
He is the only saving truth
That you will ever know.

Grasp on when life is going down,
When things seem so uncertain.
He can raise the cursed veil
Of misery's dark curtain.

Grasp on whenever choices come
And you need his direction.
The road he shows is always right
And leads you to perfection.

Grasp on and learn the love of God,
The love that runs so deep
That he would die upon a cross
So your soul he could keep.

It's never hard to grasp his hand
If you know God above.
He is your Father and your friend,
Your Savior full of love.

Psalm 138:7-8

"Though I walk in the midst of trouble,
   you preserve my life;
you stretch out your hand against the anger of my foes,
   with your right hand you save me.
The Lord will fulfill his purpose for me;
   your love, O Lord, endures forever—
   do not abandon the works of your hands."

TAKE COURAGE

Take courage, my friend and release your fear,
For the God who loves you is very near.
He'll take your hand and lead you on
And through his strength you can be strong.
He knows the pain you feel inside.
He knows the fear you try to hide.
He felt it too, when he dwelt on earth.
It's here he died to give rebirth.
The reason he can lift you now
Is because he fulfilled God's solemn vow
To save all those who come to him
Giving him their burdens when life seems grim.
So take courage because he gives you peace
And through his love you'll find release
From pain and sorrow that make you numb.
Take heart, for he has overcome!

John 16:33

"I have told you these things, so that in me you may have
peace. In this world you will have trouble. But take heart! I
have overcome the world."

HUSH AND LISTEN

In the quiet afternoon the breezes whisper through the trees,
Hush and listen, child, get down on your knees.

His presence reaches everywhere. It reaches to you now.
So hush for just a little while; humbly your head bow.

He wants to teach you patience, to wait for his commands.
He wants to teach submission, to give up your demands.

But he can only do that when you stop with listening ears
To hear his message burning in your soul with no one near.

So hush and hear his calling as he bends to touch your heart,
And let his words of wisdom in your life now have a part.

Let gentle breezes touch you, and then begin to heal.
Remember that you have a God who knows just how you feel.

Isaiah 28:23, 26

"Listen and hear my voice;
    pay attention to what I say.
His God instructs him
    and teaches him the right way."

GRIEF'S PRAYER

My heart is splitting open wide
With the burden of my grief.
The hurt continues endlessly
With no hope for relief.

And yet I know my God is there
To help to ease the pain.
He is the only one who comes
And helps to keep me sane.

The world really wants to help
But they don't understand
The great despair I feel inside.
This isn't what I planned.

So Lord, keep coming; comfort me
In lonely days ahead.
When helplessness starts crowding,
Help me look to you instead.

Help me see the reasons
For this grief within my heart.
May you be in it glorified
So life once more can start.

Psalm 34:18

"The Lord is close to the brokenhearted
and saves those who are crushed in spirit."

LIFE STRUGGLES

Life can be a struggle,
It doesn't come with ease.
Every day brings choices made,
All of which God sees.

It seems that we are pilgrims
Traveling though this life.
We must learn to journey on
While getting through the strife.

Decisions aren't all easy;
We don't know what to do.
So while mistakes come easily
Messed up lives do, too.

Yet God is ever faithful
When on his name we call.
He gives our lives direction
And lifts us when we fall.

The pain and desperation
Seem to come from far and near.
Our faith will move us onward
When his presence here is clear.

So as you travel onward
Through life's awesome tasks
Remember that he'll lead you on;
You only have to ask.

Hebrews 10:36

"You need to persevere so that when you have done the will
of God, you will receive what he has promised."

ENCOURAGEMENT

Encouragement means many things,
Things both big and small.
How can I show encouragement
When trials come to call?
Maybe a phone call or a note
To tell that I am there.
Perhaps a meal or other gifts
That show I really care.
Per chance a quick short visit,
Or a hug or smile to give.
Or just a bit of Jesus' joy
Makes life easier to live.
I must remember this each day
Preparing things to do,
Who would he call if he were here,
And help this day get through?
He told me, "Feed my children
And through you they'll see me."
So my desire is to serve him
So that Jesus they will see.
May I always be obedient
To encourage every day
The ones who Jesus shows me,
Always for each one I'll pray.
Then one day when I see him
He'll say, "Thank you, you did well.
You always fed my children.
Now come and with me dwell."

Philemon 1:7

"Your love has given me great joy and encouragement, because you, brother, have refreshed the hearts of the saints."

AT THE CROSS

My friends said, "Leave it at the cross,
That burden on your back.
For if you choose to do that
Its weight is all you'll lack."

So I knelt down before the cross
And left sorrow, shame, and guilt.
Such freedom I had never known
From towers of pain I'd built.

My life went on then joyfully
And things began to change.
I'd found relief from stressful times—
Priorities rearranged.

Yet every now and then I found
Myself controlled again
By worries come back in my life,
I'd know not where or when.

They'd sneak back very quietly
And burden me once more,
So much that I was in worse shape
Than I ever was before.

I don't know why I'd wait so long
To go back to the cross
And lay my burdens at his feet
To find all gain—no loss.

So if you're walking through this world
With burdens on your back,
Unload them at the cross today.
Find the peace and joy you lack.

Matthew 11:28-29

"Come to me all you who are weary and burdened, and I will give you rest. Take my yoke upon you and learn from me, for I am gentle and humble in heart and you will find rest for your souls."

ADVICE TO REMEMBER

Remember who you are in Christ,
Remember you're God's child.
Remember he can keep you safe
From situations wild.

Remember that he cares for you
More than others do.
Remember that he's by your side
To keep you pure and true.

Remember he gives wisdom clear,
In any situation.
Remember you can trust in him
To share life's revelations.

Remember he's forever,
He'll never fade away.
Unlike temptations of this earth
He has come to stay.

And when temptation finds you
And tries to suck you in,
Remember he's your Savior
Who died for all your sin.

The best advice I give you
Is to look to him each day.
You'll live without regrets, remorse,
If you don't forget to pray.

Proverbs 4:11-12

"I guide you in the way of wisdom
   and lead you along straight paths.
When you walk, your steps will not be hampered;
   when you run, you will not stumble."

NEVER-ENDING LOVE

Are you longing for love like no other
In a time when we celebrate love?
Are you feeling like no one will know how you feel,
And you to the side people shove?

Do you feel like there's no one around you
Who for you could ever show care?
Do you feel when you cry in the darkness for help
That you've never found anyone there?

Then for you, dear friend, I have some great news,
News that your life could be changed.
You see, Christ loves you more than anyone can.
For you God's plan was arranged.

Maybe you've never thought of a God
Who noticed you living each day.
"I'm just a mere speck in this universe.
Why should he care?" you may say.

The reason he cares is he placed you here
For a reason that only he knows.
And once you believe and accept his dear Son
His cause in your heart grows and grows.

Soon you begin to see things anew
With the joy only his eyes can see.
He can change you and make you glad.
You'll feel alive and free.

That is the news that I bring you today,
If you're living in fear and depression.
Christ takes that away. He loves you so much.
You are his prized possession.

So let him in and answer his call,
And find love only Jesus can give.
Your old self will die and fall far away,
Your new self forever will live.

Jude 1:1b-2

"To those who have been called, who are loved by God the Father and kept by Jesus Christ: Mercy peace and love be yours in abundance."

JOY IN MY HEART

My body is weary and tired today,
And I don't want to leave my bed.
But there's joy in my heart this morning
Because through God's word I've been fed.

The clouds are hiding the sun today.
The cold and the wind I can feel.
But there's joy in my heart this morning,
Because God's presence beside me is real.

The kids forgot books and lunches again
Sending me out into the cold snow.
But there's joy in my heart this morning,
Because I have the ability to go.

I have to be a mom once more
And deal with these parenting things.
But there's joy in my heart this morning,
Because God in my heart sweetly sings.

There'll be things in my day that will try me
And threaten to ruin my day.
But I'll keep joy in my heart all day long
Because God's faithful to guide all the way.

Lamentations 3:22-23

"Because of the Lord's great love we are not consumed,
        for his compassions never fail.
They are new every morning;
        great is your faithfulness."

HE HEALS THE BROKENHEARTED

Angry words and bitter thoughts
Have threatened to destroy
My sweet relationship with God
And take away my joy.

I just can't seem to understand
Why things turned out this way.
Why did my poor heart have to break
And all calm fall away?

Why are there storm clouds all around
With no light shining through?
When I look up and call for help
Why can't I just see you?

Your voice seems miles and miles away,
But my faith tells me you're near.
I know you have the words for me,
If I could only hear.

I think sometimes my heart must break
So you can reach inside
And begin to mend it from within,
And then with me abide.

Lord, may I see you and hear your voice.
Open up my ears and eyes,
So I'll understand my broken heart
And hear your sweet replies.

Psalm 147:3

"He heals the brokenhearted
    and binds up their wounds."

A FAITHFUL GOD

I have a God who is faithful.
His promises always kept.
He's carried me through rough waters,
Reassured me when I've wept.

I've found peace in most situations
Where peace might never be found.
Without his love and protection
I know in my storms I'd have drowned.

I want you to know that he never
Has failed to give me love and care.
No matter what trial I'm facing
I know that he's always there.

Whenever I've felt myself falling,
Not able to find my way back,
He's caught me in arms full of hope
And given me strength that I lacked.

His shoulders can hold all your burdens.
There's nothing that he cannot bear.
After all, he hung on the cross
And for you he chose to die there.

So be strong, my dear friend, and remember
There's never been love that gave more
Than he gave, when he carried your burdens.
His faithfulness I adore.

Deuteronomy 7:9

"Know therefore that the Lord your God is God; he is the faithful God, keeping his covenant of love to a thousand generations of those who love him and keep his commands."

HAVE YOU EVER?

Have you ever felt rejected, alone and really down?
Thinking that in this wide world there's no friend to be found?
Have you ever felt an anger when life seems so unfair,
And wondered why God lets it go and if he's really there?

Have you ever felt an emptiness that nothing seems to fill?
Wondering how you'll find his peace and how you'll know
   his will?
Have you ever felt such sadness that it seems to crush your soul,
And fervently each day sent prayer that God would make
   you whole?

Have you ever felt a bitterness destroying you inside,
Just wishing you could let it go and gain release from pride?
Have you ever felt a burden weighing heavy on your heart
And yet clung to it desperately till life soon fell apart?

Why is it that we feel these things? Why can't we let them go?
His words are there and so is he; his promises we know.
Can't we learn to turn to him in hope and faith and trust?
If we're going to survive this life, you see, we simply must.

Matthew 11:28-29

"Come to me, all you who are weary and burdened, and I will
give you rest. Take my yoke upon you and learn from me, for
I am gentle and humble in heart, and you will find rest for
your souls."

If Only You Knew

I struggled, confused by events all around.
The pound of my heart made a deafening sound.
I looked and I looked with no hope of escape.
I tried, but there just was no plan taking shape.

"I'm trapped!" I cried out in my anger and pain.
"Why would my God bring me here to remain?
It's hopeless—there's no way out that I see.
Why would my God let this happen to me?"

And as I cried out, soul full of despair,
He opened my heart and I knew he was there.

"The window is closed, so look now for the door.
Beyond it you'll find I have plans for much more.
If only you knew the love I have for you,
If only you knew that my words are all true,
If only you knew how completely to trust,
Then you would know I am holy and just.
The things you are seeing will last a short while,
And then I'll replace all your tears with a smile.
If only you knew how to hear my calm voice
I'd bring you through storms and then you'd rejoice."

I learned who to trust with my life on that day.
I learned to believe every word that he'll say.
My God is my Lord and he has plans for me,
But I have to open my heart so I'll see.

John 20:15-16

"'Woman,' he said, 'why are you crying? Who is it you are looking for?' Thinking he was the gardener, she said, 'Sir, if you have carried him away, tell me where you have put him, and I will get him.' Jesus said to her, 'Mary.' She turned toward him and cried out in Aramaic, 'Rabboni!' (Which means Teacher)."

THE RAMPART

I stand upon the rampart
And strain my eyes to see
Where God will work his mighty deeds
And what he'll say to me.

I've given my complaints to him
With earnest heartfelt plea.
Now I'll stand upon the rampart
And trust his sovereignty.

And even if the answer
Doesn't seem to fit my plan.
I'll stand upon the rampart
And trust my Master's hand.

When I can't see the answer
To all my hopes and prayers,
I'll stand upon the rampart
And remember God still cares.

Though his answer seems to linger,
I'll stand and watch each day.
For with God's love and in his time
There is no long delay.

Habakkuk 2:1, 3

"I will stand at my watch and station myself on the ramparts;
I will look to see what he will say to me, and what answer
I am to give to this complaint. For the revelation awaits an
appointed time; it speaks of the end and will not prove false.
Though it linger, wait for it; it will certainly come and will
not delay."

WILDERNESS EXPERIENCE

Lord, I'm wandering in the wilderness
That you have brought me to.
I know that while I'm wandering
You'll teach me something new.

I ask that while I'm out here
And in pain lift up my cries,
In mercy you will hear me.
Gaze down with loving eyes.

I've learned that even silence
Doesn't mean that you're not there.
Sometimes it's through your silence
That I see your loving care.

No matter where you lead me
Or the tests you choose to give,
I pray that I'll be willing
For you alone to live.

Exodus 2:23b-25

"The Israelites groaned in their slavery and cried out, and
their cry for help because of their slavery went up to God.
God heard their groaning and he remembered his covenant
with Abraham, with Isaac and with Jacob. So God looked
on the Israelites and was concerned about them."

TRUSTING THE STONE

Help me trust completely, Lord, in everything you do.
I know that all your promises are real and will come true.
So when in times of doubt and fear I need to hear from you.
Help me trust the true foundation that out of Zion grew.

A stone completely tested as he walked here day by day.
A stone that will not crumble, whatever men may say.
A stone that brings salvation, which only God could lay.
A stone that I can trust to keep my heart from all dismay.

Isaiah 28:16

"So this is what the Sovereign Lord says;

> 'See, I lay a stone in Zion,
> a tested stone,
> a precious cornerstone for a sure foundation;
> the one who trusts will never be dismayed.'"

WHAT IS FAITH?

If faith is trust in an unseen God
Then how do I know he's real?
Does this God I've never seen
Truly know how I feel?

Does he really understand
The pain within my heart?
Has he felt the hurt I feel
That's tearing me apart?

They say his Son did suffer
Upon the cross that day
That I may have eternal life
That none could take away.

But does eternal life begin
With pain upon this earth?
If faith brings me this suffering
Then what's it really worth?

I guess a faith that's sure of him
Is all I really need.
I can live with hope because
My Jesus intercedes.

There's nothing else that I can do
Except to lean on Christ.
He suffered, too, and knows my pain
For me he paid the price.

1 Peter 5:10

"And the God of all grace, who called you to his eternal glory
in Christ, after you have suffered a little while, will himself
restore you and make you strong, firm and steadfast."

PAIN, DEATH, AND FAITH

Can one through pain and veils of tears
See through the shroud of grief?
Can faith have victory over doubt
And find renewed belief?
When waves of pain come crashing in
With strong blows all around,
And hopes in peril sinking fast,
Will faith still hold its ground?
When pain within is crushing
And hampering every breath,
How will I face tomorrow,
And in faith face my own death?
One thing I must remember,
My God has suffered, too.
He felt the pain and then in faith
He died for me and you.
He knows it hurts to suffer.
I also know God's there.
In faith that's what I cling to.
I have a God who cares!

Hebrews 11:1

"Now faith is being sure of what we hope for and certain of
what we do not see."

ALL THINGS HAVE A PURPOSE

Would I be different if I could choose
Experiences in my life?
Would I have changed a lot of things
And eliminated strife?

I look back at all the times
God's given me to bear.
I see now it was in hardships
That I really felt him there.

He gave me circumstances
That I wouldn't have chosen at all.
I've lived through fear and doubt and pain,
But he's never let me fall.

Perhaps he sees much more than me
As he looks down from on high.
While I just try and understand,
He sees the reasons why.

So I'll accept the trials life brings
Assured he's doing what's best.
Experience has shown through the years
In him I can find rest.

Romans 8:28

"And we know that in all things God works for the good of those who love him, who have been called according to his purpose."

LAY HOLD OF HIS STRENGTH

I will accomplish nothing if I try it on my own.
My weakness overwhelms me as I strike out all alone.
My goals are unaccomplished without God by my side
To strengthen me and lift me, and then my life to guide.

I must lay hold of his strength to see my trouble through.
It's only through his mighty power my life can be made new.
His wondrous strength will carry me each day that I allow,
But I must lay hold of his strength, and I must do it now.

Though trials and tribulation may threaten to undo
And weaken faith in Jesus, his love will see me through.
His strength will never falter. He'll never let me down.
He'll use his strength to teach me till the day I hold a crown.

His mighty strength will come and keep me moving down
    the road.
His perfect strength will strengthen me and carry every load.
If you lay hold of his strength each day you, too, can find,
He'll lift your heavy burdens; place his peace in heart and
    mind.

Isaiah 12:2

"Surely God is my salvation;
    I will trust and not be afraid.
The Lord, the Lord, is my strength and my song;
    he has become my salvation."

PROMISES GIVEN, PROMISES KEPT

All the promises God's given
Have faithfully been kept.
Yet through the hard times in our lives
We've sorrowfully wept.

Yet our God was ever near
Providing faithful care.
God's silence speaks the most to me;
Quietly he answers prayer.

The problem's not with godly answers,
But with our own reactions
To his will planned for our lives,
Shown forth in all his actions.

I guess the choice we have to make
Is to hear or turn away
From God and all his promises
That can hold us every day.

Isaiah 8:17

"I will wait for the Lord,
    who is hiding his face from the house of Jacob.
I will put my trust in him."

NEVER FORSAKEN

Alone, but never lonely with Jesus in my heart;
I know he's always watching over me.
Sad, but not destroyed because I have a friend
Who brings me back whenever I must be.

Scared, but never fearful of things that might have been;
His perfect plan is always carried through.
Weary, but not burdened because he lifts my load
And carries me as no one else can do.

Beaten, but not broken. He always seems to keep
The pieces of my life so I can cope.
Doubtful, but not hopeless for I know, yes I am sure
That Jesus is my one and only hope.

Sinner, but forgiven for every reckless thought
That ever found its way into my heart.
Lost, but not forsaken. He swept into my life
Giving joyous love that never will depart.

Deuteronomy 31:6

"Be strong and courageous. Do not be afraid or terrified because of them, for the Lord your God goes with you; he will never leave you nor forsake you."

THE STORM CLOUD'S HOPE

I'll never understand how trials and tribulation
Can work out for my good in every situation,
The only other choice I have would be to face alone
Those trials leaving pain where my life storms have blown.

How can I trust in him when life seems so uncertain?
How can I look ahead through the storm clouds' misty curtains?
He doesn't seem to hear when I cry within my soul
To plead for his pure peace to come and make me whole.

Yet where else can I go when things are going bad?
Where else can I go when my heart's so fully sad?
The thought of leaving him to face it on my own
Brings no hope whatever when in life's storms I'm thrown.

Jesus is the rock that brings me my salvation.
There is no other hope to make me a new creation.
I know that I am his dear child to do with as he will.
It's with his joy and with his love my empty heart he'll fill.

He's caused my weary soul to fully be awakened.
Because he's by my side I never will be shaken.
My anchor will I toss for him to have complete control
When dark storm clouds of life into my being roll.

Psalm 16:8-9

"I have set the Lord always before me.
    Because he is at my right hand,
I will not be shaken.

Therefore, my heart is glad and my tongue rejoices;
    my body also will rest secure."

WITHOUT MY GOD

Where must I go to seek his face?
Where do I go to find his grace?
How can I hope to find my place
Without my God to lead me?

What must I learn before I'll hear?
What must I do to dry my tears?
How will I ever lose my fear
Without my God to heal me?

How can I hope when hope is gone?
How can I pray before the dawn?
Where can I find the living One
When darkness seems to blind me?

Where is my faith when hardships come?
Where is my joy? Why am I numb?
Why does each day begin with some
Knots of worry deep inside me?

His word tells me that I should trust.
My heart knows that I simply must.
There's no other way to clear the dust
And see his face before me.

Proverbs 29:25

"Fear of man will prove to be a snare,
    but whoever trusts in the Lord is kept safe."

A LESSON IN TRUST

Who am I trusting to guide me
Through each and every day?
Who am I gaining my strength from
Whenever I kneel to pray?

Who is watering my garden
With a spring that never runs dry?
Who am I placing my trust in
When I look up to the sky?

So often I've constantly struggled
To do things on my own,
And in those stormy trials
Hardness of heart I've shown.

When will I learn to trust God
And his Son that lives in my heart?
When will I learn to hold onto
His hand, giving all, not just part?

My head knows that it's essential.
My heart says it's hard to let go.
Please God, give me faith to remember
You love me; from my heart let trust flow.

Isaiah 58:11

"The Lord will guide you always;
    he will satisfy your needs in a sun-scorched land
    and will strengthen your frame.
You will be like a well-watered garden,
    like a spring whose waters never fail."

A Heart to Trust

BELIEVER'S REST

Did you close your eyes and sleep last night
Knowing God was in control?
Or did you lie in bed and fret,
Restless thoughts through your mind roll?

Have you given him the chance he needs
To sustain you day by day,
So when the storms of night appear
There's peace wherever you lay?

David hid within a cave one night
Writing down his Psalm.
With Absalom out for the kill
In faith he kept his calm.

God shields us and defends us
And answers when we call.
That's the way we rest in him
And into sleep do fall.

Rest within your Savior's arms
He loves you like a brother.
Those problems he can take away
For this there is no other.

Psalm 3:5

"I will lie down and sleep;
    I wake again because the Lord sustains me."

THE COMPLEXITIES OF GOD

Intricacies born out of faith in a mighty complex God
Have led me down unbidden paths where others never trod.
The network of my Father's mind is hard to comprehend.
But when I trust and walk with him I'll go where'er he sends.

Life's a new adventure beginning every day
When I follow my God's leading and let him guide my way.
I soon start to discover that I can do much more
Than I ever thought was possible, more than I did before.

It's not because I'm better than I ever used to be,
It's just because he's leading me to see the world he sees.
He strengthens me and guides me so I can do his will.
And uses me to bring new hope; my wounded heart he fills.

And when I stop and look behind to places where I've been
I'll never cease to be amazed how he carried me again.
It's always so amazing to see the way he works
And how he turns bad into good wherever evil lurks.

What I am trying to say here is you really needn't try
To figure out our complex God. He may never tell you why.
His ways are never our ways; we just don't think the same.
But I know that when he's near me, I'm always glad he came.

Let him lead you down new pathways to a distant land.
May you always go without a doubt, simply holding tight
his hand.
He's never taken me someplace where he has never been.
And the joy found on his path of life comes time and time
again.

Isaiah 55:8-9

"'For my thoughts are not your thoughts,
neither are your ways my ways,'
declares the Lord.

'As the heavens are higher than the earth,
so are my ways higher than your ways
and my thoughts than your thoughts.'"

THE SPIRIT'S GIFT

Holy Spirit, come to me and fill me with your fire.
May your presence dwell in me and fill me with desire
To know the precious Savior, who died for all my sin,
To know that by your presence here my life can now begin.

O lift me, Holy Spirit, with breath that brings me life
To free me from my burdens and relieve me from my strife.
And may I look forever to you for wisdom pure,
Not trusting self, but only you to bring my healing cure.

Protect me, Holy Spirit, from the evils I may find
That threaten to invade my soul and thus destroy my mind.
Let me walk with you instead, always by my side,
Leaning on your wisdom and your knowledge my heart guide.

Live in me, Holy Spirit, both now and evermore
Until you take me home in love and walk me through the
    door
Of God's eternal heaven where he's prepared a place
Where I can dwell in love and joy and ever see his face.

Sweet Holy Spirit, gentle One, gift of God's own grace,
Thank you for the love you send to my heart's dwelling place.

John 14:26

"But the Counselor, the Holy Spirit, whom the Father will send in my name, will teach you all things and will remind you of everything I have said to you."

A Prayer for Healing

Look to the skies! A mighty land
Is growing here on earth.
A nation young in God-timed years,
Is showing us her worth.

May this nation ne'er forget
Who lets them have each day
To do the work we're called to do.
Let's not forget to pray.

For prayer will heal the nation
From all pain and all despair.
God wants to lift our burdens
And show his loving care.

May every living person
Found in the USA
Kneel down in prayer and worship,
And may it start today.

For there's no hesitation—
I know beyond a doubt,
That God's blessed us abundantly.
We've never done without.

Dear God, hear our petitions
We bring to you today.
Please heal us and forgive us
As we bow to you and pray.

2 Chronicles 7:14

"If my people, who are called by my name, will humble themselves and pray and seek my face and turn from their wicked ways, then will I hear from heaven and will forgive their sin and will heal their land."

THE HEART OF THE MATTER

Let's go to the heart of the matter.
What's the matter with my heart?
Have I opened my Bible lately?
Each day with God to start?

I can't expect his leading
When I don't ask where to go.
How can Jesus tell me
What he wants me to know?

Will I stop what I am doing
And spend some time in prayer?
If I take the time to be near him,
I know that he'll be there.

And as for the matter of my heart
When it's opened he'll visit within.
When I'm in quiet meditation
Real matters of heart will begin.

Psalm 86:11

"Teach me your way, O Lord,
    and I will walk in your truth;
give me an undivided heart,
    that I may fear your name."

GOD'S SANCTUARY

A sanctuary I build today
With deep and reverent prayer
That God would find it worthy
To make his dwelling there.

I build it not with stone or steel
But with vast and great emotion,
To an awesome God who promises
To love with deep devotion.

A resting place I offer him,
A place that's clean and pure,
A sanctuary where he can dwell
And know his love's secure.

I offer up my mind and tongue
And every other part,
So he can dwell in peace inside
The sanctuary of my heart.

Exodus 25:8

"'Then have them make a sanctuary for me, and I will dwell among them.'"

AWAKENED

Awakened in the night,
I heard the Savior call,
"Get up and seek my heart, dear child,
Come and surrender all.

I need to spend some time with you,
To speak into your soul.
So awaken heart and soul and mind
And let me make you whole.

You struggle so with earthly things.
I need to let you know
My grace is sufficient for you,
So let other worries go.

I want to speak in the still of night
While your heart is at peace.
So wake up, listen, talk with me.
You'll know such great release.

I have these things for you to do
As you move throughout this day.
Listen to me before you act.
Read my words and pray.

Awaken, my child, and come to me,
Not just body, but heart and soul.
Awaken; be filled with my Spirit now
And I will make you whole."

Psalm 17:15

"And I—in righteousness I will see your face;
 when I awake, I will be satisfied with seeing your
 likeness."

A PRAYER FOR WISDOM

A storm cloud brews on the crest of the sea.
What will be left in its wake?
A massive destruction and hearts that are crushed,
Or honor for Christ's name's sake?

Now Satan would love it if he could divide
God's Spirit that lives in our hearts.
It gives his heart joy when a battle he wins
And Christians are driven apart.

So it's wisdom I plead for as the storm passes by.
To wisdom's lifeline I'll cling.
May I put aside selfish ambition and pride.
To my God wisdom's glory I'll bring.

Psalm 107:29-30

"He stilled the storm to a whisper;
    the waves of the sea were hushed.
They were glad when it grew calm,
    and he guided them to their desired haven."

A Heart to Pray

A BELIEVER'S PRAYER

For grace, for strength and salvation I come
To the Lord, the God of it all.
I recognize that the things that I do
Next to him are comparably small.

The Lord of all nations, the earth, and the sky,
The God of the thundering sea.
The God of the universe reigns on his throne.
I pray that he reigns within me.

I trust only him for the grace that forgives,
Only him for the strength that I need.
For salvation's hope in my heart only grows
When the God of all power plants the seed.

So grow in me, Lord, unleash all that you have
For my life, and help me believe
That all your desires and dreams for my life
From your hand to my heart are received.
Amen!

Isaiah 33:2

"O Lord, be gracious to us;
    we long for you.
Be our strength every morning,
    our salvation in time of distress."

HUNGRY HEARTS

Yearning, hungry hearts are what we really need
To focus us on Christ today in every word and deed.
If hearts are well prepared to face him every day,
We'll never need to worry about what we do or say.

For he is our example—the light that we let shine,
So others see his heart by seeing yours and mine.
Let's ask him to prepare us to serve him as we should.
Be hungry and be yearning as Jesus knew we could.

Seek him, not another, as we wake up every morn.
Hear him, not ourselves, as we seek to be reborn.
Follow only his words lived out each and every day.
Let's be hungry for the Savior in all we do and say.

Psalm 84:2

"My soul yearns, even faints,
    for the courts of the Lord;
my heart and my flesh cry out
    for the living God."

MORNING PRAYER

May the still small voice that I know is yours
Strengthen me today.
May I know what things you want of me
When I kneel down to pray.
May my heart, my eyes, my ears, my soul
Be open to all you say.
To you, my Lord, I commit my life.
To you I give this day.

Psalm 37:5-6

"Commit your way to the Lord;
    trust in him and he will do this:
He will make your righteousness shine like the dawn,
    the justice of your cause like the noonday sun."

SILENT PRAISE

In humble reverence now I come
And low before you bow.
Your awesome works your wisdom tell.
Your love your deepest vow.

In time of solitude I hear
Your holy righteous word.
Your voice comes ringing to my heart;
The sweetest ever heard.

I'll never fail to give you praise
For all your mighty deeds.
I'll come in silence to your throne.
You know my greatest needs.

The Lord is holy; listen now!
Be silent and you'll hear.
The words he speaks in silence tell
You that he's always near.

Give glory to our Father God!
Sing praises all day long!
But don't forget that to God's ear
Silence sings the greatest song.

Habakkuk 2:20

"But the Lord is in his holy temple;
    let all the earth be silent before him."

WALKING THROUGH THE DESERT

I'm walking through the desert, Lord. I chose to take this
road.
My heart is dry and parched where once your Spirit flowed.
I hate this lonely feeling when I cannot hear your voice;
So quench my thirst and fill me. Make this my daily choice.
Don't let the sands of apathy threaten to undo
The life we've shared together. Make me like brand new.
Come and rescue me, dear Lord, from my suffocating soul.
Revive me now and make me your creation pure and
whole.

Nehemiah 9:19-21a

"Because of your great compassion you did not abandon them
in the desert. By day the pillar of cloud did not cease to guide
them on their path, nor the pillar of fire by night to shine on
the way they were to take. You gave your good Spirit to instruct
them. You did not withhold your manna form their mouths,
and you gave them water for their thirst. For forty years you
sustained them in the desert; they lacked for nothing."

ABIDE IN ME

Come to my heart today, dear Lord,
And grace my humble abode.
Together our love can illuminate peace
As we travel down the road.

The thought that you, the Almighty God,
Would dwell within my being
Is almost more than I can bear.
Yet your love I'm ever seeing.

Come home, my God, and dwell within
This simple heart of mine.
Then give me strength to do your will.
May I, your light, brightly shine.
Amen

John 14:23

"Jesus replied, 'If anyone loves me, he will obey my teaching.
My Father will love him, and we will come to him and make
our home with him.'"

THE EASY LIFE

Make my life easy and do it today.
Is that what I ask whenever I pray?
Do I expect God to do things my way?
Do I really think through the things that I say?

Do my words appear human and centered on me?
Have I totally forgotten his death on the tree
So I could learn to forgive and be free?
Is all selfish thought of just me, me, and me?

Perhaps I should focus on God's way instead
And live life in joy and forget how to dread
The coming day's problems as I rise from my bed.
May I look to Jesus and trust what he said.

Psalm 40:8

"I desire to do your will, O my God;
    your law is within my heart."

DESPERATE PLEA

I reach out and desperately try hard to feel
Something I know is undoubtedly real.
I reach out in darkness with hands in the air
And try to find God through this thing they call prayer.

My heart is just bursting with all that it holds—
The pain and the agony I've tried to withhold.
If only I grasp what still lies far beyond,
If through prayer with my God I can correspond.

I know that with him there is rest and there's peace.
If I break through the barrier, I'll have my release.
Dear God, hear me calling and answer with haste.
Dear God, keep my life from running to waste.

What's that? Now I feel it, calm in my heart.
A slow, seeping joy that his Spirit imparts.
And soon all the darkness becomes holy light.
He's answered my pleas on this dark lonely night.

Praise God for the peace that he sends every time
To a chaotic world with no reason or rhyme.
Praise God for the healing that only he brings
To a heart that in pure, faithful hope to him clings.

Psalm 142:7

"Set me free from my prison
      that I may praise your name.

Then the righteous will gather about me
      because of your goodness to me."

MY PRAYER

Lord, please give me:

The unselfishness of Abraham
The strength of Samson
The courage of Joshua
The wisdom of Solomon
The trust of Noah
The faith of Moses
The peace of Mary
The life changes of Paul
The patience of Job
The sensitivity of Ruth
The boldness of Peter
The seeking heart of Nicodemus
AND the same quiet love you gave to John,
The disciple whom you loved.

2 Corinthians 9:11

"You will be made rich in every way so that you can be generous on every occasion, and through us your generosity will result in thanksgiving to God."

PEACEFUL REFLECTIONS

The sun filters golden through the great pines
Bringing bright light from heavenly glory divine.
Babbling waterfalls herald a new day.
These hills are the perfect background to pray.

So, God, bless my family, give us quality time.
May we commend your creation as these mountains we
climb.
May we find peace and rest as your nature we view.
May we never forget 'twas created by you.

Thank you for giving such beauty to earth.
We see the new flowers and animals give birth
To renew life and continue creation each year.
Thanks for the reminders—for bringing us here.

For peaceful reflections on what you have done,
May we always remember that you are the One
Who creates not just nature, but within us, too.
May we prove we're created in the image of you.

Our perfect Creator, Redeemer, and King
In this glorious setting your praises I'll sing.
You're an amazing, compassionate friend
Who'll bring me to beauty that won't ever end.

Psalm 72:18-19

"Praise be to the Lord God, the God of Israel,
    who alone does marvelous deeds.
Praise be to his glorious name forever;
    may the whole earth be filled with his glory.
                    Amen and Amen."

FROM THE HUSH OF THE FOREST

In the hush of the forest I sit and I pray.
I know God is with me each step of each day.
As I sit and observe nature passing me by
I can hear his low voice and his sweet gentle sigh.

He sits down beside me and listens with care
To all my concerns that I bring to him there.
While the sun filters through leaves on the trees
I lay out my life as I fall on my knees.

I pray to him, "Lord, you know what is best
For my life, and I trust that in you I'll find rest.
In the quiet and peace of this forest I feel
Your presence is here and I know you are real.

For all your creation cries out to the fact.
And it should determine the way that I act.
In all situations may I glorify you;
The one who listens and carries me through.

So I lay in your hands, Lord, the rest of my life.
Help me quiet my heart and give you my strife.
May I be still before you in all that I do.
May I never forget to glorify you."

Psalm 46:10

"Be still, and know that I am God;
    I will be exalted among the nations.
    I will be exalted in the earth."

HIS GENTLE WHISPER

I've seen God in thunder and lightning,
I've seen him in storms and in squalls.
But I never expected that whisper
Coming gently within my four walls.

The almighty, heavenly Father
Knelt down with me by my bed.
The King of all Kings and Creator
Came gently and there stroked my head.

He said, "Have no fear now, dear child.
My love for you is so very great
That I sent my own Son to redeem you.
Now walk with me through heaven's gate."

He kept speaking in soft gentle whispers
And implored me to let him draw near.
Sweet peace flowed from his gentle whisper
While I listened and lost every fear.

Oh, the whisper! God's gentle whisper!
The gift of his unending love.
May I listen and learn to look always
To his perfect voice from above.

1 Kings 19:11b-12

"Then a great and powerful wind tore the mountains apart
and shattered the rocks before the Lord, but the Lord was
not in the wind. After the wind there was an earthquake, but
the Lord was not in the earthquake. After the earthquake
came a fire, but the Lord was not in the fire. And after the
fire came a gentle whisper."

SIMPLE WORDS

Simple words are all it takes
To come before God's throne.
He listens to the meek of heart
And calls each one his own.

You need not know a million words
To come and plead your case.
It's simple words our Father hears
And answers in his grace.

The only thing that you must do
Is seek him every day.
He'll always hear your simple words
And guide you when you pray.

Psalm 116:6

"The Lord protects the simple-hearted;
   when I was in great need, he saved me."

PATIENCE

Grant me the gift of patience
As I'm seeking out your will.
It's one thing that I'm lacking,
The cup that I can't fill.

Why can't I ever stop and wait
For you to have your say?
Why do I want to hurry on
And move in my own way?

I need to learn to calm my soul
No matter my condition.
I need to learn to yield my heart
In complete and true submission.

For when I've done that in the past
I've found your grace and peace.
Help me wait on you, dear Lord,
In patience find release.

Psalm 37:7a

"Be still before the Lord and wait patiently for him."

THE QUIET TIMES

In the quiet of the morning I come and kneel in prayer.
I never need to worry; my God is always there.
Before the sun arises, I bring my needs to him.
He's always stopped to listen whatever state I'm in.

It's in the quiet times of life that he speaks to me the most;
When no one else can interrupt; when no one else is close.
I simply open up his Word and let it all sink in.
It's then he teaches me the most, before my day begins.

Jesus got up early to meet with God alone,
And his is my example. In all his life he's shown
That if I only look to him to help me start my day
Things will go much smoother at work, at home, at play.

And when it's really quiet, when it's just him and me,
Then I can feel his love abound. He makes it plain to see.
May I open up my Bible and ask for him to show
The things that in my quiet times he wants for me to know.

Zephaniah 3:17

"The Lord your God is with you,
   he is mighty to save.
He will take great delight in you,
   he will quiet you with his love,
   he will rejoice over you with singing."

HIS GENEROUS WISDOM

Lord, please grant me wisdom in the midst of my despair,
And show me what I have to do to bring my life repair.
You promised that if I cried out for wisdom in a storm
You'd come and speak in whispers, giving peace that's soft
    and warm.

I truly need your guidance, Lord, to show me where to go
When turmoil is attacking and those storm winds start to blow.
I seek your direction to bring me calm again.
You've promised not to take me where you have never been.

So as I start to drown in a raging tempest's blast
I pray, please give me wisdom; it's all that I can ask.
Help me see your vision as the storm clouds start to end.
Teach me with your wisdom, I'll go where'er you send.

I'll ask in faith believing and never have a doubt
That you in your great wisdom have already worked it out.
And as this trial ceases and clouds begin to fade,
I'll know you gave me wisdom from the choices that I made.

James 1:5-6

"If any of you lacks wisdom, he should ask God, who gives
generously to all without finding fault, and it will be given
to him. But when he asks, he must believe and not doubt,
because he who doubts is like a wave of the sea, blown and
tossed by the wind."

CHRIST'S STRENGTH

Is it true there's strength in you
To help me through each day?
Can I find the strength to bind
Myself to you when I pray?

Can everything I bring to you
Be done within your will?
Can I rely on you to take me
Over every hill?

Can I at length find in you strength
To overcome ordeals?
Where else can I go and always know
The strength of perfect ideals?

No one but Christ has paid the price
To take away my shame.
Strength can be mine when it's laid on the line
Because he's given me his name.

I now know to trust, I'm sure I must
If joy in my life I'll receive.
That great strength is there in his loving care.
It comes when I choose to believe.

Philippians 4:13

"I can do anything through him who gives me strength."

LOVE'S SACRIFICE

Lord, where else could I place my trust
But in your almighty hand?
You raise up the poor and help those in need.
You're a balm in a weary land.

You are great and worthy of glory.
You are great and majestic in power.
You are merciful, giving forgiveness to all.
You alone come in each needful hour.

Your love and compassion spring new each day.
You never fail those that you love.
Your holiness commands my respect.
I'll send songs of praises above.

You set the pattern for sacrifice.
Lord, you gave up your Son.
I can't understand that kind of love
That comes to a world on the run.

Dear Lord, I'm unworthy of that kind of love,
So I bow before you and pray
That you would forgive me for my imperfections
And carry all my sin away.

Lord, help me focus each day upon you
And live with the passion of Christ
In my heart to renew and grow stronger each day.
Help me, like you, pay the price.

1 John 2:1b-2

"But if anyone does sin, we have one who speaks to the Father in our defense—Jesus Christ, the Righteous One. He is the atoning sacrifice for our sins, and not only for ours but also for the sins of the whole world."

PERSEVERING PRAYER

There is a cheer from times gone by,
A cheer that you may know.
But the words should change, I think,
And this is how they'd go.

"Never give up, never give in,
Pray to win, pray to win."

It's the power of perseverance
That comes with frequent prayer.
It's one way God communicates
And let's you know he's there.

Prayer is a source of power
Some people never see.
Because they haven't made
Their prayer life all that it should be.

He calls us to a prayer life
That never seems to stop.
Those prayers if done correctly
Bring quite a fruitful crop.

Don't take this challenge lightly
Get on those knees and pray,
And learn to watch for victory
In your life every day.

1 Thessalonians 5:16-18

"Be joyful always; pray continually; give thanks in all circumstances, for this is God's will for you in Christ Jesus."

THANK YOU, LORD

You've set me free from all my prisons.
Thank you, Lord.

You love me and you've made me righteous.
Thank you, Lord.

You've brought me out of my blindness.
Thank you, Lord.

You lift me when I'm bowed with burdens.
Thank you, Lord.

You are my hope and my help.
Thank you, Lord.

You made all things, including **me**.
Thank you, Lord.

You are ever faithful.
Thank you, Lord.

May I give back a little today.
May you have reason to thank me, too.

Psalm 146:2

"I will praise the Lord all my life;
I will sing praise to my God as long as I live."

POWER IN PRAYER

Go with me today. Prepare my way,
And let me do all that you want.
I found time to pray. I love what you say.
No threat to me are Satan's taunts.

Your power is mine. I know I can find
Victory over each kind of sin.
Let me have your mind; I know Satan you'll bind,
With your help I know that I'll win.

Let me be like you, faithful and true,
Showing you to those that I see.
In all things that I do, whether many or few,
May my life with your teachings agree.

Your power is real, I know I can feel
It at work in my life every day.
Your power can heal and Satan can't steal
That power when I take time to pray.

Exodus 14:31

"And when the Israelites saw that great power the Lord
displayed against the Egyptians, the people feared the Lord
and put their trust him and in Moses his servant."

ONE DARK BLOT

There's one dark blot on my soul today;
It's the stain and darkness of sin.
One dark blot captures my heart
And keeps all my pain within.

For sin can hold me captive
From the things that God would give
To those he loves and comforts,
To the ones he's chosen to live.

It seems the sin is so deep,
Saturating my very soul.
How can my human heart conquer
What keeps from making me whole?

I understand that by myself
There's no way for me to be free,
Except through the blood of the Savior
Who came to earth to save me.

But first I have to surrender
Everything that is deep inside
And be willing to walk in his statutes
And with Jesus in my heart abide.

He'll erase the dark blot from my thoughts,
He'll erase the dark blot from my heart.
Through the power of God's Holy Spirit
Sin never need tear me apart.

Jeremiah 17:9

"The heart is deceitful above all things
    and beyond cure.
        Who can understand it?"

VICTORY

No enemy can crush you
With Jesus on your side.
He won the final victory
When on the cross he died.

For death was not the battle's end,
But victory in disguise.
To see that final victory
Just use the Savior's eyes.

When you feel all defeated
That's when Jesus works the best.
To give you strength and victory
And give your soul a rest.

It takes determination
To stay within the fight.
Don't let Satan bring you down
And keep you from what's right.

Remember who's the winner
In every Christian race.
With Jesus as your Savior
You'll always take first place.

Psalm 60:12

"With God we will gain the victory,
    And he will trample down our enemies."

ANGELS' ABANDON

The angels rise up in heaven
And with joyous abandon applaud
The fact that no man-made prison
Can keep my soul from God.

Psalm 107:10,14

"Some sat in darkness and the deepest gloom,
    prisoners suffering in iron chains.
He brought them out of darkness and the deepest gloom
    and broke away their chains."

NO CHAINS TO HOLD

There are no chains to hold me,
No prison doors closed tight
To keep me from my Savior,
The gift of grace and light.

His power, uniquely awesome,
Can break through every chain.
With one word of true repentance
He brings me home again.

For while sin's bondage over me
Seems much too strong to break,
The love of God has power
To make foundations shake.

For those who are imprisoned
And yearning to be free,
I offer Christ, the Savior,
Who holds your prison's key.

Acts 16:26

"Suddenly there was such a violent earthquake that the
foundations of the prison were shaken. At once all the prison
doors flew open, and everybody's chains came loose."

LOOK WHAT HAPPENED

The nails had left an ugly scar
On the palms of gentle hands.
The spear had pierced his precious side.
And I can't understand
The when and where, the how and why
Of all Christ did for me.
I only know it's his great love
That set my spirit free.

Look what happened, our God has done
A miracle within!
Look what happened, he has taken
Away all my sin!
I'll never know the how and why
Of what he did for me,
But look what happened, my God
Has set my spirit free.

The road he walked that fateful day,
He chose to walk alone.
It wasn't easy—what he did
To claim me for his own.
And yet he took each step in love
And died on Calvary.
Greater love can no man have.
His death proves he loves me.

Look what happened, our God has done
A miracle within!
Look what happened, he has taken
Away all my sin!
I'll never know the how and why
Of what he did for me,
But look what happened, my God
Has proven he loves me!

John 15:13-14

"Greater love has no one than this, that he lay down his life for his friends. You are my friends if you do what I command."

FROM BLINDNESS TO SIGHT

My eyes have been opened to a God full of grace.
He reached through my darkness and brought hope to
    replace
All the pain and the suffering I used to embrace.

I once was blind, but thank God, now I see.
Thank God, that he searched until he found me,
That through his mercy I now can be free.

From blindness to sight, I took the hard road.
I groped in darkness till I thought I'd explode.
Then in one gentle touch, Jesus lifted my load.

Now I no longer live a dark life in despair.
For I know my Jesus will always be there.
He's brought me to sight and released every care.
Praise God for the light found with each answered prayer!

John 9:25

"He replied, 'Whether he is a sinner or not, I don't know.
One thing I do know. I was blind, but now I see!'"

A HEART OF FLESH

Lord, I need a new heart that is in tune with you.
May the old heart melt away; my spirit to renew.

Sometimes I let humanity create a giant wall
Between my heart and what you have; I sacrifice it all.

Lord, I accomplish nothing when I do things on my own.
Why then don't I ever learn to kneel before your throne?

Your throne is filled with mercy and your heart is full of grace.
I only need a change of heart to fully see your face.

Lord, grant me your forgiveness. Let repentance come my
way.
Please give me a heart of flesh and please melt my heart of
clay.

Ezekiel 11:19

"I will give them an undivided heart and put a new spirit in
them; I will remove from them their heart of stone and give
them a heart of flesh."

GIFT OF LOVE

The gift of love God gave,
What can I then return
That's worthy of the price he paid?
He gave what wasn't earned.

A sacrifice of love
Is all I have to give
To Jesus Christ the Son of God
Who died that I might live.

Atonement now is made
For all I've ever done.
The perfect sacrifice who died
Was God's pure, holy Son.

He gave his life for me
I give my life to Christ.
I'll place him on my heartfelt throne
Because he paid the price.

Hebrews 2:17

"For this reason he had to be made like his brothers in every
way, in order that he might become a merciful and faithful
high priest in service to God, and that he might make atonement for the sins of the people."

HIS SAVING LIGHT

I wandered 'round in darkness seeking for the way
To peace and joy and happiness in all my weary days.

I looked, but couldn't find the thing I was searching for.
So I just kept on blindly knocking at each fast closed door.

Then one day just when things seemed much, much darker
than before,
I saw a door that said, "His Grace," so I knelt upon the floor.

I peeked through the tiny keyhole and saw others filled with
joy.
I knocked upon that door with all the strength I could employ.

When it opened, light flooded my soul with peace I'd never
known.
I looked and saw my Savior's face; light all around him shown.

He said, "To come in costs nothing more than faith in only me.
I am God's Son who came to earth that I might set you free."

It didn't take me very long to make my final choice.
And now each day I see his light and listen to his voice.

John 3:21

"But whoever lives by the truth comes into the light so that
it may be seen plainly that what he has done has been done
through God."

A Slave to Whom?

Who am I a slave to, myself or my dear Lord?
My freedom he has purchased; For me, his blood was poured.
So if my freedom has been bought, why do I still sin?
Why do my own desires win out time and time again?

A slave looks to his master, assured of constant care.
A maid looks to her mistress, knowing she'll always be there.
So may my eyes then look to God, my master and my Lord.
May all my life be cleansed of sin, in his mercy be restored.

Psalm 123:1-2
"I lift my eyes to you,
   to you whose throne is in heaven.
As the eyes of slaves look to the hand of their master,
   as the eyes of a maid look to the hand of her mistress,
so our eyes look to the Lord our God,
   till he shows us his mercy."

YOUR FAITH HAS SAVED YOU

Unworthy am I to bear Jesus' sweet name,
And yet he loves me always the same.
It matters not when or where I will fall.
Jesus still comes and gives me his call.

My faith has saved me from death and despair.
My faith has saved me from burdens I bear.
My heart's now no longer without his repair.
My faith in my Savior will bring me his care.

I've tried and I've failed to do right o'er and o'er.
Continually missing the blessings in store
For those who in trust and in faith will obey.
Yet Jesus, my Savior, has not gone away.

"Your faith has saved you," he tells me each day.
"Your faith saved you the day that you prayed
For me to come in and make your life new,
Your faith in me now will bring joy back to you."

I try and I fail to get rid of my sin.
I forget where I'm going and look where I've been.
But he takes my hand gently, turns me around,
And places my feet on his holy ground.

"Your faith cannot fail you if you look to me.
Remember I died and I hung on that tree.
I did it for you so that you could be free.
So focus on me and then trust who you see.

I'll love you forever, no matter what's done.
I'll love you forever because I'm God's Son.
You never need worry if your faith is true.
My love is forever and my love is for you."

Luke 7:50

"Jesus said to the woman, 'Your faith has saved you; go in peace.'"

A LONG WAY BACK

I took a little wandering way down a darkened road.
I knew it wasn't right for me, would add a weighted load.
And yet I felt compelled to move along the ruinous path.
Rebellious visions creeping in, denying aftermath.

What started as excitement soon turned into despair.
I found the promise for excitement was never really there.
And then in vain the struggle came to go the other way,
But it seemed I'd gone too far; I'd lost God's guiding ray.

So in my fear I then cried out, "Lord, please bring me back!
I'll never leave your side again. Put me on the right track!"
And then the most amazing thing came through the dark of
    night.
I saw my Savior's face shining forth through blinding light.

In grace he reached into my night and brought me into day.
I know that's where I now belong. Close by his side I'll stay.
I'll never choose another road that leads away from him.
For life is in my God alone. Without him, hope is grim.

Psalm 119:105,128

"Your word is a lamp to my feet
    and a light for my path.
And because I consider all your precepts right,
    I hate every wrong path."

SWEET FORGIVENESS

God didn't just forgive my sin, he took away my guilt.
He sent his Son to die upon a cross that man had built.
Upon the cross our Savior died up on Mount Calvary.
In pain and suffering he hung so willingly for me.
He gives such sweet forgiveness now and every time I've
   asked.
When I've acknowledged all my sin within his love I've
   basked.
Transgressions told to a loving God can clear a sin-sick soul.
Iniquities given to him make broken hearts turn whole.
So if you're feeling weary as upon this land you trod,
Release your hold on guilt and find forgiveness from your
   God.

Psalm 32:5

"Then I acknowledged my sin to you
     and did not cover up my iniquity.
I said, 'I will confess
     my transgressions to the Lord'—
and you forgave
     the guilt of my sin."

REDEEMED

At the cross I know I'll find deliverance from my sin.
At the cross I know I'll find no savior that's like him.
Jesus is my perfect friend, there's no one else I know
Who comes whene'er I need him most and goes where're I go.

Who else would ever die for me before I gave him love?
Before I even lived on earth he came from up above
To complete God's perfect plan for all humanity.
He lived and died to purify all my iniquity.

He carried every dirty sin that I have ever done.
Upon his back he placed them to complete what he'd begun.
No matter what I thought I'd done or how bad those things
    seemed,
He simply placed them on his back and said, "You've been
    redeemed."

So now I come back to the cross to find my joy and peace.
It's at the feet of Jesus Christ I find such sweet release.
I know that when he died for me, he also died for you.
If he could change me inside out, he can change you, too.

Titus 2:13-14

"While we wait for the blessed hope—the glorious appearing
of our great God and Savior, Jesus Christ, who gave himself for
us to redeem us from all wickedness and to purify for himself a
people that are his very own, eager to do what is good."

MY CORDS VERSUS HIS CORDS

Restrained in life by cords of sin that I have not untied,
I cannot do it on my own. I know because I've tried.

Some days the cords seem tightly bound with no hope for
    release.
Some days it seems I search and search with no hope for
    God's peace.

The cords of sin often threaten to take the life within
If I don't quickly come in prayer and give him all my sin.

He felt the cords upon his wrists bound in Gethsemane.
Those cords were tied on sinless hands all because of me.

If I could do it on my own and never sin again,
He would not have to die for me, my victory to win.

My cords verses his cords; one brings pain; one makes us free.
He let them tie those cords because he loves both you and me.

And now we're free from binding pain if we will seek his face.
He gave us all that he could give. He gave amazing grace.

Psalm 129:4

"But the Lord is righteous;
    he has cut me free from the cords of the wicked."

GOD'S PROTECTION

God protects his children who live upon this land.
He watches over every one; upholds them in his hand.
If you're one of his chosen, one of those he loves,
You never need to fear him or his judgment from above.
He shelters you in mercy, and in his loving embrace.
You have no need to fear him; you can always find his grace.
If you look to him as Father, and seek his will to do,
Then God, your Abba Father, will give his heart to you.
It costs no earthly treasure to be one of his own.
It comes simply with surrender to the God upon his throne.
I pray you've come to know him and love him in every way.
So your Father God will keep you, and guide you when
you pray.

Malachi 3:17

"'They will be mine,' says the Lord Almighty, 'in the day when I make up my treasured possession. I will spare them, just as in compassion a man spares his son who serves him.'"

SWEET RELEASE

Lord, I lay my heart before you giving everything I own;
To you, dear God, it's laid before your throne.
For I know that every blessing that I have ever had,
Has come from the pure grace of you alone.

And there's sweet release, oh Father God, simply in letting go,
As I place both joys and worries at your feet.
And there's sweet release, oh Father God, because I now
do know
That you'll guard my heart till one day when we meet.

Lord, I wish they knew what I know, how you always lift
me up,
Always taking all my burdens and my cares.
On your precious, caring shoulders, you've carried me
before,
Not denying me when sorrows must be shared.

It's sweet release, oh Father God, to trust alone in you,
Always knowing that no one can love me more.
There's sweet release, oh Father God, in simply knowing you,
Looking forward to my time on heaven's shore.

Lord, your heart is pure and perfect; I wish that mine
were too,
So I ask you now to cleanse me deep within;
So I'll be an empty vessel, one which only you can fill
And I'll feel that sweet release from all my sin.

There's sweet release, oh Father God, please, please let me
    come
Into your presence, Lord, to sing and praise.
You're sweet release, oh Father God. I give you all my love,
And forever to your name my praises raise.

Luke 4:18-19

"The Spirit of the Lord is on me,
    because he has anointed me
    to preach good news to the poor.
He has sent me to proclaim freedom for the prisoners
    and recovery of sight for the blind,
to release the oppressed,
    to proclaim the year of the Lord's favor."

WHITE AS SNOW

In my life is a feeling of joy
Because I've been washed white as snow.
Where filth and destruction once lived in my heart,
Now my sweet Jesus I know.

He came to my life through his powerful love,
Shedding blood on the cross for all men.
All defilement and dirt have now been removed,
And my heart is clean once again.

As the sun reflects on the new fallen snow
Sending glittering rays that blind,
So the Savior reflects light into my heart
Removing the sin left behind.

I see all the snow lying over the ground
Covering every small part of the earth.
I know Jesus died to cover my sins,
When he did so, he showed me my worth.

Psalm 51:7

"Cleanse me with hyssop, and I will be clean;
wash me and I will be whiter than snow."

CRUCIFIED WITH CHRIST

I've been crucified with Christ.
What does that really mean?
Did I bear a heavy cross
And two thieves then hang between?

I was never sinless
Or good enough to be
A holy sacrifice for God
Till Christ came into me.

Those thorns of sin I placed there
Upon his holy brow
Left me shame and desolation
Which he took away somehow.

When I was crucified with Christ
My old self died there too.
Those sins were all washed clean away
To make my heart brand new.

When I think of the magnitude
Of what he did that day,
I vow to crucify desires
That steer me from his way.

Lord, help me please stop sinning
So that your work upon the cross
Will mean what it was meant to mean,
And won't be for a loss.

Galatians 2:20

"I have been crucified with Christ and I no longer live, but
Christ lives in me. The life I live in the body, I live by faith in
the Son of God, who loved me and gave himself for me."

WINTER REFLECTIONS

The snow lies gleaming on the ground
Reflecting the sun's rays.
Do I stand gleaming before God,
Reflecting his Son's ways?

Righteousness is a gift from God,
That makes me clean within;
And pure and new and wholly his,
And completely free from sin.

It comes to me through Jesus Christ,
My life he has restored.
He made me clean and white as snow.
For me his blood was poured.

There was no other sacrifice
That was good enough, you see;
For Jesus is the perfect one
And he was blemish-free.

So on this winter day may I
Reflect upon my shame
That he so freely carried
To the cross, my soul to claim.

Ecclesiastes 9:1a

"So I reflected on all this and concluded that the righteous
and the wise and what they do are in God's hands."

HIDDEN TREASURE

There's treasure in my heart today
That's hidden deep within.
A gift from God he's given me
To keep me free from sin.

No other joy I've ever known
Brings so much peace and grace
Than this that's treasured in my heart
That brings me to this place.

Some hidden treasures can't be shared,
But this one's not like that.
The more I give away each day,
The more he gives me back.

I gave control of all I have,
To receive this thing so dear,
To Christ whose wisdom brings new life;
So now I need not fear.

I wish that all the people who
Are living on this earth
Could find this treasure that I have;
I've gained it through rebirth.

Matthew 13:44

"The kingdom of heaven is like treasure hidden in a field. When a man found it he hid it again, and then in his joy went and sold all he had and bought that field."

LIGHT THROUGH THE DARKNESS

There's darkness in our world today
That kills the souls of men.
It creeps in unsuspectingly
Time and time again.

Its shadow falls o'er all the earth
To come and steal away
Each person's claim to joy and hope,
Making empty each new day.

Where can we turn to save ourselves?
Is there any place at all?
Can we turn our futile world aright
And thus prevent our fall?

Thank God he didn't put us here
With no hope of finding light.
His brightness burns all dark away
And gives us back our sight.

So open up your eyes today
And let his Son shine in.
You'll send this world's black night away
When you cleanse your heart from sin.

John 1:4-5

"In him was life, and that life was the light of men. The light shines in the darkness, but the darkness has not understood it."

VICTORY'S PROMISE

The wind howls through my spirit, Lord,
Convicting me of sin.
Why do I keep on failing
Over and over again?

I know you taught grace and mercy.
I know your promise is true.
So why don't I just remember
To turn over temptation to you?

God, please teach me your perfect ways,
Correct me when it needs to be done.
Force me to learn to trust in you
So my victory will be won.

There's victory in the power of your blood.
There's victory in your name.
Lord, when I choose to yield to you
There's victory there to be claimed.

Thank you, Lord, for the victories
You bring to me each day.
Thanks for your grace and mercy
I find when I kneel down and pray.

1 Corinthians 15:57

"But thanks be to God! He gives us the victory through our
Lord Jesus Christ."

PRIDE BEFORE THE FALL

Some people seem to go through life convinced they have
    it all.
And all too soon it seems they find, pride goes before a fall.
They spend their life so busy gathering in the worldly things,
Like cars and boats and houses big and lots of diamond
    rings.

It's sad that they don't understand what life is all about.
They simply go along each day without a fear or doubt.
But God will judge their actions whether now or in the end.
He is the righteous judge whose perfect guidelines never
    bend.

Folks continue on the slippery path to destruction and a fall,
Never realizing that with Christ they could have had it all.
Their present life is just a dream that soon will pass away,
And then it will be all too late, like sunset's ending ray.

They will waken from the dream that man placed in their heart
And find it was not real at all; their lives have come apart.
An instant end to happiness; an eternity of dread,
Because they never placed Christ first to guide them on ahead.

God can only guide a heart who listens to his call
And daily yearns to do his will and thus to have it all.
My prayer is that he'll find in you a heart that he can stir,
So you'll not waken from a dream of things that never were.

Psalm 73:18-20

"Surely you place them on slippery ground;
    you cast them down to ruin.
How suddenly are they destroyed,
    completely swept away by terrors!
As a dream when one awakes,
    so when you arise, O Lord,
        you will despise them as fantasies."

THE POWER OF HUMILITY

Christ's time on earth was soon to end,
Each moment ticked away.
There seemed so much left yet to do
Before that final day.

Disciples still were struggling
With concepts great and small.
One area of deep concern
Was who was best of all.

So Jesus taught a simple thing
By his great illustration.
He taught them deep humility
Was not beneath their station.

He washed the feet of everyone,
Including his betrayer.
He must have looked to Judas' eyes
And offered up a prayer.

For even now there was a chance
That Judas would come home
And hold on fast to Jesus' hand,
Nevermore to roam.

But Judas made a choice that day
To follow Satan's lead,
And be led to kill the Christ
Who would not intercede.

And even though he thought he'd won
When Judas turned his back,
Satan never realized
The power that he lacked.

For God can take a Judas
And use him for His glory.
For final judgment is the Lord's,
And that's the greatest story.

Still Jesus serves with love and joy
And washes each one's feet
Who humbly comes to give him praise
With sacrifices sweet.

Yes, our Lord was crucified
And, yes, he rose again.
He lives in heaven victorious.
Death's battle he did win.

John 13:2-5

"The evening meal was being served, and the devil had already prompted Judas Iscariot, son of Simon, to betray Jesus. Jesus knew that the Father had put all things under his power, and that he had come from God and was returning to God; so he got up from the meal, took off his outer clothing, and wrapped a towel around his waist. After that, he poured water into a basin and began to wash his disciples' feet, drying them with the towel that was wrapped around him."

THE SPARROW SONG

The sparrow sings his praise each day
To the one who gives him life.
With joy the melody flows forth
Without a hint of strife.

The sparrow doesn't seem to care
What worries lie beyond.
He simply lifts his head and sings
A carefree, joyous song.

The sparrow doesn't take the time
To scheme and plot and plan.
Instead he places daily needs
Into his Master's hand.

The lesson from the sparrow's song?
Quit thinking, "Why?" and "How?"
The lesson from this tiny bird
Is trust your Savior now!

Matthew 10:29-31

"Are not two sparrows sold for a penny? Yet not one of them
will fall to the ground apart from the will of your Father.
And even the very hairs of your head are all numbered. So
don't be afraid; you are worth more than many sparrows."

THE FIXER UPPER

I looked at the house displayed in the ad
Which said "Good for the handy man,
A real fixer upper for those with a will
To bring beauty wherever they can."

And then I began to think about me
And the house I offered my Lord.
Am I a fixer upper too,
Just waiting to be restored?

If I am to be a temple of God,
A place for his Spirit to dwell,
Then I must make my heart his home
And restore this empty shell.

I'll clean all the corners and tidy up
The places neglected so long.
I'll be cleansed and purified once more,
My heart forgiven all wrong.

When I find myself remodeled
And pleasing in his sight,
I'll keep working on his temple
By living a life that's right.

2 Corinthians 6:16b-c

"For we are the temple of the living God. As God has said:
'I will live with them and walk among them, and I will be
their God, and they will be my people.'"

CONSIDER THE ROSE

Consider the rose, a most perfect flower,
A symbol of love and God's unlimited power.
From the deep seeded roots to bloom looking above,
The rose is a symbol of eternal love.

With roots so well grounded in God's nourished soil,
So like works of God bringing fruit to my toil.
I, too, in God's word should be grounded so deep
That the fruits of my faith will seem natural to reap.

The stem supports thorns, blossoms, and leaves,
Just as God will sustain and hold those who believe.
The rose leaf blows gently and follows the wind.
Can I follow his Spirit; go where he will send?

And what would a rose be without every thorn
To keep the shrub humble with those spines that adorn?
Indeed like the rose, thorns enter my being
To humble my thoughts, to him send me fleeing.

At last comes the glory, the superb, crowning bloom
That enters a place and dispels every gloom.
Perfection like that at last will come near
When I flawlessly reach my Lord Jesus so dear.

May I be like the rose so well-nourished with care,
And strive to touch heaven and see my Lord there.
Like the rose and its bloom may I search every sky
And wait for his coming to take me on high.

Zechariah 8:12

"The seed will grow well, the vine will yield its fruit, the ground will produce its crops, and the heavens will drop their dew. I will give all these things as an inheritance to the remnant of this people."

PETER'S GIFT

'Twas the third time that the cock crowed when Peter realized
That he had betrayed his Master and declared his name
    despised.
Oh, the horror that then gripped him as fell upon his knees
And in anguish wept in shame and so to God put forth his
    pleas.
"Dear Father, please forgive me for all those things I said.
It's just as if I nailed the nails and placed thorns on his head.
For when I did deny him, I also denied you.
I stand condemned before you, God. Do what you must do."
But later Jesus rose to life as master over death.
He walked among believers; taught them faith with every
    breath.
Then through his words the women brought to Peter Jesus'
    gift.
"Tell all the twelve, and Peter too." He healed denial's rift.
Now Peter knew without a doubt that Jesus loved him still.
Forgiveness came and Peter's soul the Spirit came to fill.
From that day on, Peter walked in boldness with God's power
Proclaiming Jesus' name with joy until his final hour.

Mark 16:7

"But go, tell his disciples and Peter, 'He is going ahead of you
into Galilee. There you will see him, just as he told you.'"

A Spider's Perseverance

The spider weaves her web and moves with grim determination.
She slowly plans and weaves some more in making her creation.
And oftentimes the winds will blow and take her from her
    task,
But she never stops or spends her time to in the sunshine bask.
She plods along at steady pace not noticing distractions
As forward on the silky strand she moves with ruled reactions.

What lesson can we learn from such an insect so minute
That relentlessly completes her work determinedly mute?
It's perseverance that I see in the web that she just wove.
It's what I also need to learn as through my life I rove.
And when I find that winds of life have thrown me off the
    course,
I, too, must crawl back on my web and move without remorse
Until my task is over, accomplished by his will.
The spider and me, our webs all done, experiencing life's thrill.
It's only with completion and with a look behind
We'll see the rainbow on our web and see where God did shine.

James 1:4
"Perseverance must finish its work so that you may be mature
and complete, not lacking anything."

METAMORPHIC CHANGE

From cocoon to butterfly, a change wrought by God's hand.
From deep within, the change becomes sheer beauty as God
  planned.

It's an ungrasped mystery of life how he can bring such change,
And yet, he has created all, the good, the bad, the strange.

Could metamorphic change come and create new life in me?
Could he change me deep within to what he wants for me to be?

How would that change then come about from tin to precious
  gold?
How can my heart be changed to be beautiful and bold?

And yet his change is gentle for he'll change in subtle ways
The one who bids him enter. He'll change the one who prays.

Psalm 51:10
"Create in me a pure heart, O God,
  and renew a steadfast spirit within me."

THE RENEWAL OF SPRING

Oh, the bliss of knowing that it's finally spring.
I love when the birds their new songs start to sing.
I love what the new days full of promise now bring.
I love how the warm winds dispel winter's cold sting.
Butterflies emerge with a song on their wings.
The flowers, their petals to the sky seem to fling.
A much bluer sky contrast kites on the string.
Happy people all know the new season will bring
The renewal of life that comes only in spring.
Yet we can't forget who brings these new things,
Like robins and tulips and kids running on wings.
It's by God's mighty hand creation does ring.
Praise to the Creator, our Savior and King.

Genesis 1:14-15

"And God said, 'Let there be light in the expanse of the sky
to separate the day and the night, and let them serve as signs
to mark seasons and days and years, and let them be lights
in the expanse of the sky to give light on the earth.' And it
was so."

PILATE'S DILEMMA

What shall I do with this man called Jesus?
What shall I do with this Nazarene?
That was the question Pilate was asking
Before he washed his hands clean.

The problem with Pilate is that he forgot
To wait patiently for the reply.
If he'd waited he'd know that Jesus was Christ.
Instead he sent Jesus to die.

Since then many people have asked the same question,
And many have not really found
The solution as to what to do with the Savior
Whose words seem so profound.

If only they'd quiet their hearts for an answer.
If only they'd wait for his Spirit.
They'd know what to do with this man called Jesus.
They'd know his presence, not fear it.

For Jesus will never walk far away
From a soul who is searching for him.
He'll open his arms and draw each one near.
All questions of life will grow dim.

So what will you do with this man called Jesus?
Reject him or live by his grace?
Pilate rejected and sent him away.
He sent him to die in your place.

Matthew 27:22

"'What shall I do, then, with Jesus who is called Christ?'
Pilate asked. They all answered, 'Crucify him!'"

WHAT IS FAITH?

To be sure of what we hope for and what we do not see,
To know that God is for us, that's faith. It is life's key.
We know he formed the universe with only one command.
He made it out of nothing with one stroke of his hand.
By faith Cain brought his offering and gave God all his best,
While Abel kept the good stuff and gave to God the rest.
By faith Enoch went to heaven. God took him straight away.
He never felt the sting of death. Faith took him home one day.
Noah's fine example of faith was in the ark.
God judged the world, moved the boat; on Ararat did park.
Father Abraham got a call to leave his earthly home.
In faith he found the Promised Land and never more did roam.
God then gave Abe a family; though he was good as dead.
He was the "dad" of millions, a patriarchal head.
There also followed Isaac, Jacob, and Joseph, too.
They all had faith that God would finish what he said he'd do.
Moses, with the grace of God, in faith led Israel out
Of Egypt to the Promised Land. He never had a doubt.
Many others followed suit; in faith, they did believe.
Even though their lives were hard, God did their souls relieve.
They bear an affirmation of faith for me and you.
Our faith in God's pure goodness will always bring us through.

Hebrews 11:39-40

"These were all commended for their faith, yet none of them received what they had been promised. God had planned something better for us so that only together with us would they be made perfect."

THE TAPESTRY

Upon examining my needlework,
I became painfully aware
That though the top looked wonderful,
On the bottom knots were there.

The top was woven, if I must say,
Into a marvelous sight to behold.
The bottom was ugly and quite a mess.
It already looked worn and old.

Then I remembered an illustration
A friend of mine once shared,
How God was weaving a tapestry
Of our lives; not a stitch would be spared.

The knots and tangles were needed, you see,
For without them the stitches won't stay.
And the tapestry would just fall apart
Without knots being put there today.

When God looks down on life's tapestry
He sees from up above.
He sees the whole beauty of creation
In us that he's fashioned in love.

So don't let the knots and the snags of life
Give you reason to despair.
Just let the master weaver work
As your life he weaves with care.

Psalm 139:13-14

"For you created my inmost being;
    you knit me together in my mother's womb.
I praise you because I am fearfully and wonderfully made;
    your works are wonderful,
      I know that full well."

THE HUMOR OF CREATION

God has a sense of humor,
It's really plain to see.
Who else would make an aardvark,
Then turn and create me?

He worked nonstop for six days
And then he took a rest.
Then looking out o'er all the world
He saw he'd made the best.

His favorite creation
Placed in the paradise
Was Adam and Eve, his people;
From dust they did arise.

God has a sense of humor,
But he also had a plan.
We could be his children
If we just took his hand.

Have you reached for your Creator
And let him work in you
His magic of creating
To change you through and through?

Genesis 1:31a

"God saw everything that he had made and indeed, it was
very good."

THE HUNDRED-FOLD HARVEST

A sower sowed some seeds one day
With planting time in spring,
Hoping a harvest one hundred fold
The reaping in fall would bring.

Alas! Some fell upon the path
And quickly they were trodden.
Others fell on shallow ground.
They grew, but were soon forgotten.

The thorns and roots choked other seed.
The sower grew distressed.
His hopes for harvest one hundred fold
Soon fell; his faith digressed.

But lo and behold, believe it or not,
Some seeds took root and grew!
They brought forth fruit one hundred fold.
Believe it because it is true!

So the sower kept on sowing
Each spring, because he had learned
That to reap a harvest one hundred fold
You must plant while expecting to earn.

Matthew 13:8

"Still other seed fell on good soil, where it produced a
crop—a hundred, sixty or thirty times what was sown."

MIRACLES ON DEMAND

You can't expect our God to do his miracles on demand.
That's what the Pharisees found out; it wasn't what they planned.

They told him, "Show us something great, never seen before,
A lightning flash, a giant wave come crashing on the shore."

But Jesus sadly shook his head, "You simply do not get it.
The only sign you'll get from me is this, and you'll regret it.

I'll spend three days like Jonah spent in the belly of a whale,
But not in a fish, in the heart of the earth, will thus begin my tale.

It happened on the third day that the whale threw Jonah out.
So it will be with me, too, I'll be raised without a doubt.

Even then you will not get it because you are so blind,
Letting Satan and his evil ones control your tight-closed minds.

But those who wait patiently let me work in my own way.
My time is always perfect. I'll not lead them astray.

They don't demand a miracle; they just look into my eyes
And see each day's small miracles unhidden, undisguised."

Matthew 13:16-17

"But blessed are your eyes because they see, and your ears
because they hear. For I tell you the truth, many prophets and
righteous men longed to see what you see, but did not see it,
and to hear what you hear but did not hear it."

THE TROUBLE WITH PHARAOH'S HEART

Pharaoh's heart was very hard, in fact as hard as ice.
He wouldn't let those Hebrews go. He wasn't very nice.
Pharaoh's heart was also cold. He acted without feeling.
The result he found, to his surprise, was frogs upon his ceiling.
Though Moses warned repeatedly that Pharaoh'd never win,
That Jehovah was the Lord of all, he just would not give in.
So rivers of blood and locust plagues were cast upon the land.
Hail and boils, gnats and flies when Moses raised his hand.
Their cows were dead, their sheep were, too, and darkness
    replaced light.
Yet Pharaoh stubbornly refused to do what he knew was right.
So God was left without a choice. Old Pharaoh'd made it clear
He'd never let God's people go and lose those slaves so dear.
So God prepared his people, with Moses as their guide,
And gave them strict instructions from the plague of death to
    hide.
They placed blood upon their doorframes, ate lamb and
    unleavened bread
And listened to the wailing of those with firstborn dead.
The plague of death passed over every Hebrew old and young.
But Pharaoh's son was dead now. The plague of death had
    stung.
He finally called for Moses. "Get your people out of here!
Take silver and gold, whatever. Just leave our lives in the clear!"
The caravan began moving. Pharaoh was glad to see them go.
God sent a pillar of fire and cloud, his way of direction to
    show.
Soon Pharaoh missed his workmen. His contracts were
    getting behind.

So he sent his men after Moses to see what they could find.
But God protected his people now that they were free,
And led them away, but Pharaoh's men were drowned in
   the Red Sea.
So what's for us in this story? Do you think that it could be
To soften our hearts towards Jesus, so like Moses, God's
   power we'll see?

Hebrews 11:24-25

"By faith Moses, when he had grown up, refused to be
known as the son of Pharaoh's daughter. He chose to be
mistreated along with the people of God rather than to
enjoy the pleasures of sin for a short time."

A WALK OF FAITH

Jesus sent his disciples out to row across the lake.
They didn't know a storm would come and put their lives
at stake.

But he had not abandoned them to a watery grave,
So he walked out on the water with assurance their lives to
save.

Then Peter jumped impulsively from the safety of the boat,
And began to walk to Jesus while his faith kept him afloat.

But the wind began to scare him and he took his eyes away.
As he sank in desperation he remembered, "Now it's time
to pray!"

So he yelled, "O Lord, please save me!" And he reached for
Jesus' hand.
Then Jesus reached and grabbed him; it wasn't like Peter
planned.

He thought his faith was stronger and he sadly looked about
When Jesus had to ask him, "Why were you filled with
doubt?"

Yet the others had only sat there holding tight onto their
oars,
Watching in silent amazement, listening to the waves' dull
roars.

Then he silenced the waves and the water; the wind was
quieted, too.

The disciples bowed down in worship as their faith began
to renew.

Have you kept your eyes upon Jesus, not daring to look far
away?
Because Jesus will keep you from drowning if you focus on
him every day.

Matthew 14:32-33

"And when they climbed into the boat, the wind died down.
Then those who were in the boat worshiped him saying,
'Truly you are the Son of God.'"

THE LESSON OF JOB

What can I learn from the life of Job,
A blameless man upright?
He shunned the evil of this world
And was worthy of praise in God's sight.

He was the greatest of all the men
In the East, in the land of Uz.
He prayed for his children early each day.
He did it for them just because.

He was blessed with riches and worldwide fame.
God had given him the best.
Then Satan came from around the world
And asked to give Job a test.

So God said, "OK, but don't take his life,"
And Satan gave Job extreme pain.
Job lost everything—possessions, respect,
It looked like no hope for regain.

His friends came along to give him advice,
Some good, but most of it bad.
Job questioned his life, sought answers within
Until he thought he'd go mad.

Then out of the storm God finally spoke
To teach Job wisdom and strength.
And Job learned to lean on God's mighty arms
Through testing, whatever the length.

Job learned to trust in no one but God,
As God is who God should be.
His thoughts are not ours; we can't understand
How he works for you and for me.

So with lesson learned, God finally restored
His blessings to Job through the years.
He'd learned that God teaches in every storm
And renews us after the tears.

Job 23:10

"But he knows the way that I take;
    when he has tested me, I will come forth as gold."

LOVE AND FAITHFULNESS

For the love and faithfulness we share
Through the union of man and wife,
I thank the Lord for every day
You've been a part of my life.

I know my love has been your strength,
As your love has been mine.
The safe security of our love
Has stood the test of time.

When no one else could understand
I knew I'd find you there
To take my times of broken heart
And ease my deep despair.

Thank you, Love, for writing me
On the tablet of your heart.
Though time has passed, in many ways
Each day's a brand new start.

For from this moment onward
I'll claim my love for you.
With the faith we have and the love we share
Our God will see us through.

Proverbs 3:3

"Let love and faithfulness never leave you;
    bind them around your neck,
        write them on the tablet of your heart."

AN ANGEL TO SPARE

Lord, could you spare an angel today
To carefully guard my child?
To keep her protected and safe from harm
In a world that's often defiled?

Could you send an angel alongside her today
To quietly whisper your word?
When she needs to respond to the voices she hears
May your voice above all else be heard?

Could you send an angel to guard her heart
From senseless and meaningless pain?
The world can be cruel outside of your love.
I pray that her heart be unstained.

Lord, could you spare an angel today?
You know I can't always be there.
But help me remember that you're there, dear Lord.
I entrust her to your loving care.

Matthew 18:10

"See that you do not look down on one of these little ones.
For I tell you that their angels in heaven always see the face
of my Father in heaven."

A PRAYER FOR AMERICA'S CHILDREN

Lord, I pray for America, and ask that you would send
Healing and forgiveness and all hatred to its end.
May we in love portray your grace to people one and all.
May other nations look to us as breaking down that wall.

Lord, I pray for peaceful hearts filled with love and joy.
For children growing in our land, for each small girl and boy.
They are tomorrow's promise of hope within our land.
May each one reach and touch a life guided by your hand.

Sometimes it seems so hopeless, yet we dare not give in
To quiet desperation. We see where we have been.
And we can learn from years gone by to make the future bright
For every little boy and girl. We can't give up the fight.

They have no one to look to except the leaders here
That you have placed in government. The situation's clear.
Lord, give our leaders wisdom and lead them in your way
So we can give the children hope to carry on someday.

Lord, please save the children, our nation's future light.
Keep them all protected in your loving sight.
Give them your clear vision of where we go from here
That they may save the nation, Lord, which we hold very dear.

Isaiah 11:6

"The wolf will live with the lamb,
      the leopard will lie down with the goat,
the calf and the lion and the yearling together;
      and a little child will lead them."

TO BE LIKE A CHILD

Lord, give me the heart of a child
So trusting, loyal and true,
Believing all that you tell me
With a faith refreshing and new.

Give me the mind of a child
Like a sponge soaking up each new thing
That your words speak as they teach me.
Let my mind to your wisdom cling.

Give me the feet of a child
So willing to follow your way
In obedience without question or doubting,
Never dreaming you'd lead me astray.

Give me the hands of a child
Learning by trial and error
To complete every task that you give me,
Never forgetting to begin each with prayer.

And, Lord, give me the faith of a child
Seeking only to know what is true,
Showing others the kingdom of heaven
In all that I say and I do.

Matthew 19:14

"Jesus said, 'Let the little children come to me, and do not
hinder them, for the kingdom of heaven belongs to such as
these.'"

A PRAYER FOR FATHERS

He's set down an example, our Father up above,
A plan laid out deliberately, and given forth with love.
He's shown the perfect method to guide a father's course,
So he can face the pilgrimage with no cause for remorse.
The love God gives to them each day he gives without condition.
May every father hear his voice and give the same rendition.
Lord, give each man who has a child the true desire to be
The kind of father you have been as you have fathered me.
May each look to you alone for guidance every day.
May each look to you with faith and not forget to pray
For every child you've given and placed within his care.
Lord, help each dad to not forget that you are always there.
Lord, give them great enduring strength as trials come their way.
Uphold them with your mighty hand and by their side please stay.
May they always trust in you when facing life's demands.
This task you've given fathers and placed within their hands.
May they illustrate your life for children everywhere,
As you have set before each dad a case for loving care.
Give each father aptitude to set the spiritual tone
Within each family and each house as they search for you alone.
Dear God, you so loved Jesus, your precious, firstborn Son.
Through him you gave great victory, the final battle's won.
Help fathers always trust you with faith that's born of love,
Remembering your Son, the King will guide them from above.

Proverbs 14:26

"He who fears the Lord has a secure fortress,
  and for his children it will be a refuge."

TO MY DAD

Some things never change it seems
And, Dad, you're one of those.
As I was struggling to grow up
You kept me on my toes.

You taught me faith and honesty
And values far above
The ones I learned from other folks.
You taught them out of love.

Your quiet strength sustained me
When turmoil didn't subside.
I never had a fear for life
When you were by my side.

I learned hard work and loyalty
Weren't taken very lightly.
I learned to look to God above
And hold to his hand tightly.

You did the usual father things,
The fishing trips were fun.
But more than that you made our home;
Your work was never done.

So now I want to thank you
For all you did for me.
You lived your faith and passed it on.
That faith has set me free.

Proverbs 17:6

"Children's children are a crown to the aged,
and parents are the pride of their children."

A FATHER'S TRUST

Thank you, Dad, for all you've done
To help me through the years.
You've given me your love and care
And often dried my tears.

We've shared our little secrets
That no one else will know.
You've always been a steady rock
When life dealt heavy blows.

You always gave your full support
And gave me all your best.
Even when the times were hard
You never stopped to rest.

You taught me honesty and faith,
To stand up on my own.
You taught by your example,
Your trust in God you've shown.

You taught me I should trust in God,
For that I do thank you.
There've been times I've had to trust.
Thank God, you taught me to.

Psalm 22:4

"In you our fathers put their trust;
    they trusted and you delivered them."

STAYING IN THE LINES

Driving down the road one day my child said to me,
"What does God use to color the world? Is it markers or
   paint we see?"

I responded as a mother should, "God uses anything he finds."
Her response right back I'll never forget, "Well, he sure stays
   in the lines."

It made me think as I journeyed on, how far I've really strayed
From the guidelines for my life, I know that he carefully laid.

How many times have I stepped out and tried things on my
   own
When I should have searched within his word for teaching
   he has shown.

How much easier my life would be if I had stayed within the
   lines
And let him lead me day by day following his roadmap's signs.

Proverbs 3:6

"In all your ways acknowledge him,
   and he will make your paths straight."

A TALE OF BOWLING ANGELS

I looked outside my window,
My heart was filled with fear.
I'm always apprehensive
When stormy clouds draw near.

Then I turned around and saw
An unassuming child.
My little girl had come downstairs
And looked a little riled.

"The angels are bowling again," she said,
"They're making too much noise.
And I can't sleep. I might as well
Go play with all my toys."

The golden hair flowed softly
Around her pouting face,
But what struck me was her lack of fear.
It's true! There was no trace.

She simply knew that up on high
The angels were having fun,
Creating the thunder by bowling too much.
She'd not sleep till they were done.

I learned a lesson well that night
From a child who seemed so small.
I'd have to give my fear release
And let God have it all.

So now I've learned to trust him,
Although sometimes I fail.
I remember the bowling angels
And the lesson of their tale.

Philippians 4:6-7

"Do not be anxious about anything, but in everything, by prayer and petition, with thanksgiving, present your requests to God. And the peace of God, which transcends all understanding, will guard your hearts and your minds in Christ Jesus."

A MOTHER'S TEARS

The mother clutched her child's robe.
It was all that she had left.
Her husband gone, her son was dead,
Her heart in pain bereft.

The tears flowed softly down her cheeks
As they carried him away.
The coffin held her future hope,
And they were burying it today.

And as she grieved the Lord came by,
He looked into her eyes.
His heart went out and touched her soul.
He told her, "Please, don't cry."

"Your child will live, he will be healed.
I'll bring him back to you.
His life will mean more than before
For all that you've been through."

"For through his suffering you will see
The Father glorified.
And others will cry out to God
Because your child died."

He touched the coffin, held the boy,
Returned him to his mother.
The people praised the Lord in awe,
Rejoicing, hugged each other.

For Jesus was in their midst that day
Bringing faith in God above.
A mother's tears were turned to joy
Because of Jesus' love.

Luke 7:13

"When the Lord saw her, his heart went out to her and he said, 'Don't cry.'"

MOTHER ROBIN

I've observed a mother robin feeding her young.
She diligently feeds them the food from her tongue.
Backwards and forwards again and again,
Her task goes forever; it seems with no end.

No matter how much she brings them to feed
It seems they want more; they have such a great need.
Yet she never gives up nor slows down her flight.
She perseveres on, flies from ground to the heights.

No one taught her to give loving care
To her young ones and yet she's always been there
To nourish, protect, keep them safe with her wing.
At night a lullaby, sweetly she'll sing.

You see, it's our Father that's made her so wise
That she knows how to comfort her little ones' cries.
He cares for each bird and each living thing.
Whether great or small, they are under his wing.

So we need not worry when things seem grim.
We must trust our Father; rely only on him.
If he cares for each robin and knows each small bird
Then know that he loves you, your pleas he has heard.

And there is none other who'll give you such care
As God, our great Father, who dwells everywhere.
Trust him and trust him and trust him some more
Till you feel his love burning your soul's inner core.

Psalm 50:11

"I know every bird in the mountains,
and the creatures of the field are mine."

TO MY MOM

When I think back on those days long ago
From childhood till now, I continue to grow
And I think of my mom and all that she did,
And the things that she gave up just for me, her kid.

My mom at the clothesline or holding a hoe,
Or snuggling me tight at the town picture show.
My mom at the sink or the sewing machine
Making sure we had clothes and that we were clean.

My mom in the garden or else at the stove
Canning or baking—for perfection she strove.
She taught me to sew, cook, bake, love, and share.
It's by her example I learned how to care.

Holding her black Bible in church oh so tight,
I'll always remember with love that sweet sight.
It all started there with my mom in that pew,
My love for a Savior so loving and true.

I'll try to pass on, Mom, all that you taught
To my own little ones and give them the thought
That Jesus is Lord, and Savior, and King,
His love in their hearts, his salvation they'll sing.

Proverbs 31:28

"Her children arise and call her blessed;
　　her husband also, and he praises her."

A MOTHER'S PRAYER

Lord, could you guard the heart of my child,
Keep her safe and secure within?
Could you place your hedge all around her today,
Making sure she'll not hurt again?

Lord, how I love this child you've given.
I've protected her safe in my arms.
But no matter how hard I try and I pray,
I can't keep her from all of life's harms.

But you, Lord, are mighty and full of love.
I know I can trust her to you.
You love her more than ever I could.
So through you may her life start anew.

God, no one else knows the way that you do
What it's like for your child to see pain.
Your Son felt it, too. Was it as hard for you?
Did you weep the day he was slain?

Lord, I realize now I can't take away
My child's pain and her tears,
But, Lord, remind me that you know how I feel.
You, too, felt your child's pain and fear.

And yet through that pain there was victory too,
As he came back to life just to give
A promise of hope and a life with no tears.
Thanks to your child's pain, mine can live.

Revelation 7:17

"For the Lamb at the center of the throne will be their shepherd;
he will lead them to springs of living water.
And God will wipe away every tear from their eyes."

My Gram

When I was just a little girl we traveled to see my Gram.
My wonderful great-grandmother who made great bread
and jam.
She always had a smile waiting and yummy cookies, too.
Those memories she created, I wonder if she knew.
We slept out on her screened-in porch in the heat of a
summer's night.
We always felt safe and soundly slept in the streetlamp's
glimmering light.
One of the memories I have of her is so precious I'll never forget.
She sat in her rocker and read from her Bible and showed
no signs of regret
Of the time which she could do something else I thought
would be more fun.
But she just kept on reading by the light from the afternoon sun.
She sat and read, rocked back and forth and finally I said,
"Why do you read that book so much? Let's do something
else instead."
But Gram just smiled and looked at me with wisdom gained
with age.
"I learn more about my future home by reading every page.
I want to find out all I can so that when I'm finally there
Things will be familiar to me. I'll know I'm in heaven so
fair."
Pretty soon after that, Gram became ill, and then she
eventually died.
My mom shared the news with all of us kids. I remember
how much I cried.

But I also recalled my Gram in that chair reading her Bible
with care.

I knew in my heart that she was OK; she now lived in
heaven so fair.

She taught me the need to study God's word and know
where my future will lead.

Now I'll know my Lord's voice and also his face because on
his word I did feed.

May I teach my children, in love and with joy, the
importance she taught to me,

The truth of God and of his holy word that will set my
children free.

Deuteronomy 4:9

"Only be careful, and watch yourselves closely so that you
do not forget the things your eyes have seen or let them
slip from your heart as long as you live. Teach them to your
children and to their children after them."

MY MOTHER'S QUILT

My mother made a quilt for me.
She made it scrap by scrap.
When it was placed upon my bed
It showed my life's road map.

My life was sewn there, piece by piece
Into that lovely quilt,
And the memories of my life it seemed
Lovingly were built.

There was my favorite party dress
And there my sister's skirt,
My brother's operetta suit
And there his cowboy shirt.

Some colors bold and beautiful,
But others ugly seemed,
Yet put them all together
And beauty from them streamed.

Now life to me is like that quilt:
Each piece is good or bad.
Each memory brings back a day,
Some happy and some sad.

But God can take each tiny scrap
And piece it just so right
That when life's quilt is finished
It's a glorifying sight.

His favorite piece to sew, I think,
So beautifully in place
Is the one where we accept his gift
And come to him in grace.

Philippians 1:6

"Being confident of this, that he who began a good work in you will carry it on to completion until the day of Christ Jesus."

THE LEGEND OF THE LIGHTHOUSE

A lonely ship was passing
Through the dark and starless night.
The wind pushed hard at every turn
No end of strife in sight.
The captain tried to steer the ship
To the safety of the shore,
But wind and rain and black of night
Kept his path from comfort's door.
He struggled past the coastline,
Where danger lay in wait.
Hidden rocks and bladed cliffs
Seemed filled with deadly hate.
His only hope of finding peace,
Or a haven in the night
Was to look toward the coastline
And see the lighthouse light.
Standing high above the rocks
With unwavering, steadfast hope,
Was the lighthouse shining brightly
Down the craggy, rocky slope.
The light remained a constant,
An unfailing source of life
That kept the ship from sinking
And the captain's heart from strife.
Its light shone forth its beacon
Through the dark and dreary night.
Its light sent forth that word of hope
And kept the ship aright.

One life can touch another,
Bringing hope to one soul's fight.
One life can touch another,
Giving light through darkest night.
The legend of the lighthouse
Lives not just on rocky shores.
That light of hope shines brightly
Through hearts with open doors.

Luke 11:33

"No one lights a lamp and puts it in a place where it will be hidden, or under a bowl. Instead he puts it on his stand, so that those who come in may see the light."

THE SHOULDERS OF A SHEPHERD

The shoulders of a shepherd
Bear a heavy weight.
To lead the flock of God
Is a task that oft seems great.
While sheep are often stubborn
And very hard to lead,
The shepherd keeps his focus
And prays for every need.
A shepherd's shoulders often bend
With the burden of it all,
For trials come and bring their pain,
Some great and then some small.
A shepherd hears the Father's voice
And seeks to do his will.
He brings each case before the Lord,
He listens and is still.
A shepherd has no easy task
In leading Jesus' sheep.
Into his hands their lives are placed,
His privilege to keep.
A reminder to the shepherd,
Whose shoulders may feel weak;
You don't bear the flock alone
When your Father's will you seek.
Lean on the other Shepherd
Who taught you all he could,
So that your shoulders can be used by God
The way he knew they would.

Take courage, gentle shepherd,
The Lord is on your side.
He'll give you strength and wisdom
As you let him be your guide.

Luke 15:4-6

"Suppose one of you has a hundred sheep and loses one of them. Does he not leave the ninety-nine in the open country and go after the lost sheep until he finds it? And when he finds it, he joyfully puts it on his shoulders and goes home. Then he calls his friends together and says, 'Rejoice with me; I have found my lost sheep.'"

THE EYES OF CHRIST

I saw the eyes of Christ one day in a little child's face.
His hands were covered in filth and grime. He looked so out
    of place.
His ragged clothes, the way he smelled, the language that he used
Disgusted me, I turned away not knowing he'd been abused.

I saw the eyes of Christ one day in the eyes of a homeless man.
Leaning up against the wall, eating food from a tin can.
How sad, I thought as I passed him by that he must live that way.
So I walked on not knowing that he'd die the very next day.

I saw the eyes of Christ one day when I visited the nursing home.
A lady in the hallway looked so lost and all alone.
"Too bad her family doesn't come and cheer her up," I said.
I didn't know till later that her family all was dead.

I saw the eyes of Christ one day near me in the church pew.
I smiled and shook her hand and said, "Hello, it's nice to see you."
I thought, "She has it all together, she seems so free from strife."
How was I supposed to know that week she'd end her life?

And then one day it happened to me, disaster fell like rain.
I looked and looked into other eyes, wanting them to see my pain.
They smiled and laughed, and went their way, unable to even see
My hurt, my pain, and what it meant, and what it did to me.

And suddenly I realized that I was that way, too.
"Oh, Lord," I prayed, "I know it now – those people, they were you!
You've taught me a valuable lesson of life and now I realize
I must walk with my heart open, so I won't miss your eyes."

Matthew 25:40

"The King will reply, 'I tell you the truth, whatever you did for
one of the least of these brothers of mine, you did for me.'"

FORGIVE HOW?

Do What? Forgive as Christ forgave me?
I could never possibly do that!
The wrongs done to me have hurt so much,
Every lie I've had to combat.

My enemy ruined my reputation,
And took away my friends.
And after it all, he still runs me down.
When will it ever end?

I tried to amend and talk it all out,
But his shoulder was turned on me.
For too long a time this has broken my heart.
How I long to be set free!

But forgive him for all the pain he has caused?
Why me? I've done nothing wrong.
Why should I be the one to forgive?
He's carried this out for too long.

Yet you say, Lord, "Forgive as I forgave you
The day that Jesus was slain."
I won't cheapen the work that you did on the cross.
I'll forgive and my freedom regain.

Colossians 3:13

"Bear with each other and forgive whatever grievances you may have against one another. Forgive as the Lord forgave you."

The Follow-Up Lesson

You have a sense of humor, Lord.
Today you made me smile.
You challenged my heart yesterday
To go the extra mile.

You had a lesson there for me
I really had to learn.
Forgiveness goes to everyone
Even when it isn't earned.

And so I chose to obey you
And forgave the way you asked.
The bitterness was swept away
And in your joy I basked.

I do my part and you do yours—
The partnership's divine.
I thank you, Lord, for teaching me.
I thank you that you're mine.

Colossians 3:25

"Anyone who does wrong will be repaid for his wrong, and there is no favoritism."

THE EXAMPLE

What am I willing to give up today
To keep my brothers from sin?
How can I keep my heart focused on God
So their spiritual journey won't end.

My prayer is that I keep looking above
So a stumbling block I won't be.
My heart would be torn if I caused anyone
To fall and be distanced from Thee.

So I sacrifice whatever I must
To set Christ's example for living.
It will not be hard, for the joy that will come
Is found in the beauty of giving.

1 Corinthians 8:9

"Be careful, however, that the exercise of your freedom does
not become a stumbling block to the weak."

To My Friend

A friend is just a friend, but you are so much more.
You've taught me lessons for my life I never knew before.

You've given me yourself in so many different ways.
You've given love and patience and your heart's enduring
    praise.

You're always there to lift me up whenever I feel low.
Your encouragement has meant a lot; more than you'll ever
    know.

And so the challenge for me today is simply to try and be
The very special kind of friend that you have been to me.

I'll always try to listen if you ever need me to,
Because a friend loves at all times. You've taught me this is true.

Proverbs 17:17a
"A friend loves at all times."

THE NATION'S HARVEST

This land will yield its harvest
And then we will be blessed
With hope and restoration
And much sought after rest.

God's given us protection
When we have gone his way.
He's blessed us with abundance,
Enough to give away.

He's given mighty power
And placed it in our hands.
He gave responsibility
To help less fortunate lands.

America has its beauty
That comes from God alone.
His work will be fulfilled here
With guidance from his throne.

We pray for further blessings
Upon this land we love.
May God forever help us
And guide us from above.

Psalm 67:6

"Then the land will yield its harvest,
    and God, our God, will bless us."

THE NEED FOR SALT AND LIGHT

The light of the world? The salt of the earth?
Is that what I've been since I gained new birth?
Have I let my light shine to the people next door?
Or is it hiding within so they can't see any more?

Help me remember they need to see you.
Help me to show them in all that I do.
I pray that my words would bring salt and light
As I seek to bring others near to your sight.

May I be much saltier and shine so much more
Than I've ever been able to shine before.
May the way that I live make them want to know you.
May they learn to praise you through the things that I do.

Matthew 5:13,16

"You are the salt of the earth. But if the salt loses it saltiness, how can it be made salty again? It is no longer good for anything, except to be thrown out and trampled by men. In the same way, let your light shine before men, that they may see your good deeds and praise your Father in heaven."

GO AND SPEAK

"Speak and let them hear my words
That they can know my truth.
Go and let them feel my love
That they gently can be soothed.

Help each one to know me more
And thus their lives fulfill.
Guide them using what I give
That they may know my will.

Say what I command you to
And never fear it's wrong.
Do for those who need me most
So they'll know where they belong.

But first make sure your heart is right
So you can hear me speak.
Be cleansed and whole, with heart renewed
So that you can help the weak".

Jeremiah 1:6-7

"'Ah, Sovereign Lord,' I said, 'I do not know how to speak;
I am only a child.' But the Lord said to me, 'Do not say, "I
am only a child." You must go to everyone I send you to and
say whatever I command you.'"

WHY FORGIVE?

If God forgave us and made Christ our brother,
Then why can't we learn to forgive one another?
The deep, bitter hurt that we hide in our hearts
In time and with nurture will tear us apart.

And that's not the plan that God has in store.
When we learn to forgive we can find so much more.
Our time on this earth will vanish like mist,
So open your heart and unclench your fist.

Replace hate with love and then find God's peace.
Replace pain with joy and find God's release.
We must learn to give ourselves over to Christ.
In forgiveness for us, he paid the ultimate price.

Colossians 3:13-14

"Bear with each other and forgive whatever grievances you
may have against one another. Forgive as the Lord forgave
you. And over all these virtues put on love, which binds
them all together in perfect unity."

FOR MY HURTING FRIEND

Lord, my friend is hurting today.
Whatever can I do?
Show me how to help her, Lord.
Teach me to be you.

I know I can't remove her hurt
Or take away her pain,
But send me, Lord, to help her trust
That she'll be whole again.

Heal her soul, Lord. Start today,
And if you can, use me.
Please give her love and courage, Lord.
Your face I pray she'll see.

Heal her, lift her, help her, Lord,
Get through this painful time.
Hold her as she seeks your peace
When in your arms she climbs.

Until the healing time is done
I'll lift her in my prayers.
There is no better way to show
How much that we both care.

Isaiah 40:1

"Comfort, comfort my people,
    says your God."

My Purpose

What is my purpose here on this earth?
Why have I come to be?
To open their eyes and turn them to light
That they might come to see.

God sent me here not to look in myself,
But to reach much further beyond.
To touch other hearts and bring them to Christ,
Help them to his love respond.

The forgiveness of sin is a gift that I've found
That's too wonderful not to share.
And the joy that it brings through faith in our Lord,
To nothing else can compare.

So spread it around as we're all meant to do,
This gift of our Father's grace.
Then his light will go forth, his glory be revealed,
As reflected through your human face.

Acts 26:17b-18

"I am sending you to them to open their eyes and turn them from darkness to light, and from the power of Satan to God, so that they may receive forgiveness of sins and a place among those who are sanctified by faith in me."

MORTAL VERSUS IMMORTAL

I am just a mortal traveling through this land.
My time on earth soon slips always, washed away like sand.

There is no way to measure time the way my Father does.
So life becomes uncertain, never staying like it was.

And while I know that I can look ahead to life above,
Those around don't recognize his hope or feel his love.

They think they are immortal, that their life will never end.
So they hurry through each day not knowing Jesus as their
friend.

A meaningless existence for their lives it seems they've made.
And in the end they'll find how far from grace they've really
strayed.

So if I, then, could teach them all the secret of success,
'Twould be to live a mortal life and in God's word find rest.

Psalm 116:8-9

"For you, O Lord, have delivered my soul from death,
  my eyes from tears,
  my feet from stumbling,
that I may walk before the Lord
  in the land of the living."

A CULINARY LESSON

They'd come to Jesus to report
On what they'd taught in every port.
These twelve disciples, simple men,
Had come to tell him where they'd been.
He said, "Come now and rest with me
And tell me all the things you've seen."
So they did, but it wasn't long
Before the crowds to him did throng.
With compassion, and lack of sleep
He looked with love upon these sheep.
They seemed so lost and so forlorn.
Souls were broken; hearts were torn.
He selflessly began to teach
Hoping many hearts he'd reach.
Soon the time passed quickly by
And supper time was drawing nigh.
The disciples tried to send away
Those sheep that Jesus taught that day.
But he told them instead to feed
The sheep that seemed so much in need.
"But, Lord, we have no food to give.
Send them home to where they live."
But Jesus told them, "Look around,
See what you find upon the ground."
They brought two fish, five loaves of bread—
Not much to feed five thousand head.
But Jesus put them all in groups.
The twelve disciples made the loop

And fed five thousand; every one!
And food was left when they were done.
The task complete, he sent them home
And went to pray and be alone.
They learned a lesson there that day:
With Christ you'll always find a way.

Mark 6:41-44

"Taking the five loaves and the two fish and looking up to heaven, he gave thanks and broke the loaves. Then he gave them to his disciples to set before the people. He also divided the two fish among them all. They all ate and were satisfied, and the disciples picked up twelve basketfuls of broken pieces of bread and fish. The number of the men who had eaten was five thousand."

AROUND EVERY CORNER

I looked 'round the corner and I saw Jesus there
To teach me to live the way I'd never dare.
To boldly live life to its fullest extent,
To live life like Christ is my highest intent.

As I see Christ in people I meet every day
Around every corner, may I watch and pray
To live like he did as he walked on this earth,
Making people feel loved and know their true worth.

As he walks with me now, I just want to be
Christ to all people, each one that I see.
May I never forget everything that he did
So that I in the shelter of his wings can be hid.

And I want other people, it matters not who,
To know that this Jesus loves them that much too.
But in order to do so I must try to see
Christ around every corner to teach and guide me.

For I can't take them farther than I've been myself.
I can't live by faith if my faith's on the shelf.
Around every corner I'll look and I'll seek
For his pure example to be humble and meek.

Isaiah 41:9

"I took you from the ends of the earth,
from its farthest corners I called you.
I said, 'You are my servant';
I have chosen you and have not rejected you."

A MELTED HEART

Lord, the ice and the snow are melting away
Now that winter is finally ending,
And the promise of life is out there today
As spring's first signs you are sending.

Along with the spring comes an air of hope
That winter had almost suppressed.
Through winter's cold void you helped me to cope
And in you I was able to rest.

But, Lord, like the ice there are many sad hearts
In the world that are still very hard.
Each one every day from your good word departs,
The ice in their hearts turns to shards.

I know only you can melt that hard ice
And restore each sad heart to its whole.
Lord, give me the chance to give your advice
That you might today save a soul.

The melting of hearts comes from you and your love.
Make me your agent of care.
Together we'll tell of your Son's power from above
And the way hardened hearts he'll repair.

Psalm 147:18

"He sends his word and melts them;
    he stirs up his breezes, and the waters flow."

JUDGMENTAL JUDGING

I think God's word is very clear
When it comes to judging others.
Be sure what's in your own back yard,
Before judging your sisters and brothers.

There's nothing in this whole wide world
That causes more distress
Than Christians judging Christians,
Each one thinking they're the best.

That's Satan's work, he tries his best
To cause the church to split.
The sound of Christians in conflict
Is the sign of a direct Satan hit.

Nothing gives him more pleasure
Than seeing Christians fight.
We argue over details small
Convinced that we are right.

Now don't we all seem foolish
To nonbelievers far and near?
We give them cause to doubt the Lord
While Satan stands and cheers.

So Christians, please remember
We've important work to do.
We all must work together
To make God's dreams come true.

Luke 6:37-38

"Do not judge and you will not be judged. Do not condemn, and you will not be condemned. Forgive, and you will be forgiven. Give and it will be given to you. A good measure, pressed down, shaken together and running over, will be poured into your lap. For with the measure you use, it will be measured to you."

FRIENDSHIP IN GOD'S KINGDOM

There's sweet friendship in God's kingdom;
It's friendship like no other.
It's because of his love that's within us,
We've become like sister and brother.

I know that his plans are perfect.
'Twas his plan that brought us here.
I'm thankful to him that he did that
Because to my heart you've grown dear.

Please know that you'll always find here
A special place within my heart.
Whether you're near or you're distant
My love will never depart.

Thank you for all that you taught me
And the growth that you brought me as well;
The challenge to not be complacent,
But to others God's love I will tell.

Go knowing because you've been with me
I've experienced much change in my life.
I'm stronger and wiser than ever.
You gave a spirit that revived.

I pray for you joy and contentment
With God's leading to show you the way.
I pray for you vision and wisdom,
That God's presence you'll feel every day.

And someday when we are in heaven
I know that we'll joyfully meet.
We'll sing glory and laud in his presence
And gather in love at his feet.

Hebrews 2:11

"Both the one who makes men holy and those who are made holy are of the same family. So Jesus is not ashamed to call them brothers."

FROM THE SHEEP TO THE SHEPHERD

With God as my Shepherd leading each day
There's no hope of turning to be led astray.

He shelters me in the fold of his arms
And keeps me safe from life's foul harms.

Through his vigilant care every need is met.
He died for me and he paid my debt.

Oh, glorious Lord, with grateful heart
I thank you that I've been set apart.

I am your sheep; I know your voice,
Forever grateful I made that choice.

I rest secure on your shoulders strong
And let you carry me all day long.

John 10:11

"I am the good shepherd. The good shepherd lays down his
life for the sheep."

THANK GOD HE CAME

He came to bring joy. He came to bring peace.
And we can thank God he gave us release
From a world full of sin and hopeless despair.
Yes, we can thank God that he'll always be there.

Thank God for the baby he sent down to earth
To give hope to the hopeless and life through his birth.
Thank God for the plan that he put into place
When his small infant Son came to die in disgrace.

O dear Father in heaven, I can't understand
How you humbled your Son; sent him as a man.
How he emptied himself of all glory attained,
Dying there on the cross; with my sin he was stained.

While I can't understand why you did it that way,
I'm forever grateful for the work done that day.
You died just for me, so that I can have life.
Thank God for your sacrifice easing my strife.

The only thing now to do is for me
To accept Jesus' work done on Calvary.
It's only through love that he could have died
So that I could eternally with him abide.

Philippians 2:8

"And being found in appearance as a man, he humbled himself and became obedient to death—even death on a cross!"

THE MERCY OF OUR GOD

Praise God for his grace and his mercy,
For his love that overflows.
Praise God for unending forgiveness,
For his love that won't let go.

A mighty and powerful God we have,
Yet one with a heart so mild.
He judges our sin and changes our hearts,
Then in mercy he calls us his child.

The way he forgives and restores us
Is something that we don't deserve.
But in his great love for each child of his heart
He redeems us, our souls he preserves.

So with humble heart we bow before God
And lay every sin at his throne.
Then in mercy and love and because we have faith,
God forgives us and makes us his own.

Titus 3:5-6

"He saved us, not because of righteous things we had done,
but because of his mercy. He saved us through the washing
of rebirth and renewal by the Holy Spirit, whom he poured
out on us generously through Jesus Christ our Savior."

THE FAITHFUL FATHER

You bring sunshine to a soul
That's darkened with pain,
And you bring joy to a heart
Where no hope remains.

You bring peace to a life
Where turmoil abounds,
And you bring songs of rejoicing
Above all earthly sounds.

For who of us, Father,
Can ever repay
Your faithfulness given
So freely each day?

May we all be faithful
In all that we do
So that when others see us
They see a reflection of you.

2 Corinthians 3:18

"And we, who with unveiled faces all reflect the Lord's glory,
are being transformed into his likeness with ever-increasing
glory, which comes from the Lord, who is the Spirit."

ENTIRELY HIS

There is such a joy deep down in my soul,
Of being complete and totally whole.
A fullness, a peace—do you know what it is?
A knowledge that I am entirely his.

There comes such a peace with knowledge of this,
A release from worry, a feeling of bliss.
For God reconciled himself to me when
Jesus died on the cross for me and all men.

For God's precious Son hung in shame and disgrace.
He took all my sins and he died in my place.
His blood sacrifice mingled there with his love,
So I could belong to my God up above.

Entirely his for now and always.
Entirely his for the rest of my days.
Unbelievable mercy the Lord's given me.
I'm his and so glad that I'm forever free.

Colossians 1:19-20

"For God was pleased to have all his fullness dwell in him,
and through him to reconcile to himself all things, whether
things on earth or things in heaven, by making peace through
his blood, shed on the cross."

SACRIFICE OF GRATITUDE

I come to him with humbleness and heartfelt gratitude.
He paid a debt I can't repay and gave new attitudes.
It's freedom that I feel today with God's pure guarantee.
He took my sins upon the cross; in mercy set me free.

How can I repay the debt that's so long overdue?
He made atonement on the cross. He died for me and you.
Nothing that I have on earth can ever satisfy
The debt I owe to Jesus Christ for his willingness to die.

The gratitude that I feel should cause me then to lead
A life that's pleasing to the Lord in every word and deed.
A sacrifice of gratitude I lay upon his altar
Because he gave his love to me, and his love never falters.

Leviticus 17:11

"For the life of a creature is in the blood, and I have given it
to you to make atonement for yourselves on the altar; it is
the blood that makes atonement for one's life."

My Debt

God doesn't owe me anything.
I owe him everything.
And so I humbly come and bow,
To him my debt I bring.

In grace and in his mercy
He heals and he forgives.
The reason that he does that?
It's in my heart he lives.

No one can love me stronger,
No one will give me more.
I'll be forever grateful
That he entered my heart's door.

In humble adoration
With grateful attitude
I always will remember
Who gives my spirit food.

From dust he did create me,
To dust I will return.
I'll live each day for Jesus,
Repaying what I earn.

Isaiah 54:10

"Though the mountains be shaken
    and the hills be removed,
yet my unfailing love for you will not be shaken
    nor my covenant of peace be removed,
      says the Lord, who has compassion on you."

A CARPENTER'S LOVE

He was just a carpenter who lived in Galilee,
But that carpenter chose to die and hang upon a tree.
And miracle of miracles, he did it all for me.
It was his perfect love that so completely set me free.

How could a simple carpenter give such amazing grace
To us who often shun him and refuse to give him space
Within our hearts so hurried by our lives' full hectic pace?
It was his love that caused my sin to flee without a trace.

I've known no greater love that ever came from any man
Than Jesus Christ of Nazareth showed through God's perfect
    plan.
To be the perfect sacrifice, God's ultimate demand
Laid out with great precision way before earth's time began.

Praise to the humble carpenter and to his Father, too.
Have you realized the things they gave up just for you?
One gave his life, one gave his Son to guide our whole life
    through.
Thank God for his Son, the carpenter, whose love has made
    me new.

Isaiah 25:1

"O Lord, you are my God;
    I will exalt you and praise your name,
for in perfect faithfulness
    you have done marvelous things,
    things planned long ago."

A HEART FULL OF LOVE

Lord, my heart is filled with love
As I pause to reflect on your gifts from above.
The moon and the stars all lift you in praise.
I will worship you through all of my days.

The clear, blue sky signals endless space.
Your infinity baffles the human race.
It's awesome to know that you're in control
As days on this earth continue to roll.

I watch the clouds as they go drifting by.
Even they follow your course chosen on high.
So, Lord, may I, too, follow your chosen path
And thus avoid your righteous wrath.

I praise you and thank you for infinite grace,
And pray you'll sustain me till I see your face.
In the meantime, help me to choose what's right,
So I can shine as I walk in your light.

Isaiah 28:29

"All this comes from the Lord Almighty,
       wonderful in counsel and magnificent in wisdom."

MY WALK WITH GOD

How can I walk on with God if I'm standing in one place?
How can I know the way to go without looking for his face?
"I walk with God," I've often said to those to whom I talk.
But am I truly walking, or do I just talk, not walk?
To walk one must go forward, never looking back.
To walk I must surrender and trust for what I lack.
Each day should be a challenge for me to grow in Christ.
I can't negate the life he gave; I know he paid my price.

Deuteronomy 5:32-33

"So be careful to do what the Lord your God has commanded you; do not turn aside to the right or to the left. Walk in all the way that the Lord your God has commanded you, so that you may live and prosper and prolong your days in the land that you will possess."

MY CHOICE

What is the cost to follow Christ? What must I give up?
Do I need to die for him to drink his righteous cup?
What does the Lord expect of me when I then make that
    choice
To follow him in every way, have I given up my voice
In how I run my life from here? What does it really mean?
What things must I let loose of to be considered clean?
I know I'll face rejection, because he said I could.
I know life won't be easy; he never said it would.
So why in heaven's name should I give up everything I own?
That's it! It is for heaven's name he'll someday take me home.
I will never have to hunger for my food, sleep, peace, or rest.
Because I have his promise that he'll give me all the best.
If that's the cost to follow him then I have no need to choose.
Because there is no choice at all; I win or else I lose.
And I choose winning over death into a fiery grave.
Thank you, Lord, for all you've done and how my life you
    saved.

Deuteronomy 30:19-20

"This day I call heaven and earth as witnesses against you that
I have set before you life and death, blessings and curses. Now
choose life, so that you and your children may live and that
you may love the Lord your God, listen to his voice, and hold
fast to him. For the Lord is your life and he will give you many
years in the land he swore to give to your fathers, Abraham,
Isaac and Jacob."

HE GAVE IT ALL

Until I value what Christ did for me on Calvary
My life won't please him very much; I'm not what I should be.

He willingly surrendered life unto his Father's will.
He made himself as nothing so my life he could fulfill.

He never lost his kingly power or his authority.
He simply laid it to the side and hung upon that tree.

And even in that time when he was being crucified,
His majesty and might were there, they couldn't be denied.

He gave it all, pushed self aside to die on Calvary.
He gave it all. I know he did it out of love for me.

He gave it all. There's nothing more that he could ever do.
He gave it all. Because he did, my life is made brand new.

He gave it all, gave everything. What does that mean for me?
That I should live as he did, and then I can be free.

Matthew 26:53-54

"Do you think I cannot call on my Father, and he will at
once put at my disposal more than twelve legions of angels?
But how then would the Scriptures be fulfilled that say it
must happen in this way?"

ONLY A STABLE

'Twas only a stable on a dark, quiet hill
That cradled a babe on a night cold and still.
While stars gently glistened through darkness that night,
A stable held the glory of God's holy light.

The birth of the Christ child had just taken place.
The reflection of God brightly shone from his face.
That tiny red face would bring love to the world.
But for now humbly slept, in his mother's arms curled.

Mary and Joseph looked down with awe
At God's new creation and loved what they saw.
For God sent a miracle in his quiet way
To a small, lowly stable on a hill far away.

Is your heart a stable prepared from within
To cradle the King who can free you from sin?
Are you prepared to make Jesus your own?
Has your heart's stable become Jesus' throne?

Isaiah 16:5

"In love a throne will be established;
 in faithfulness a man will sit on it—
 one from the house of David—
one who in judging seeks justice
 and speeds the cause of righteousness."

WHAT DID MARY SEE?

What did Mary see when she looked at the tiny fingers curled
so tightly about her own? Did she know that those tiny
appendages would grow to…

Caress the face of a man born blind?
Love those the world had left behind?
Hold the scrolls and challenge the mind?
What did Mary see?

Did she see the change in lives he touched?
The leper he healed from desperation's clutch?
Did she see the world that he loved so much?
What did Mary see?

Did she know these fingers would five thousand feed?
Or teach twelve men to go forth and lead?
That he'd teach and encourage by his words and deeds?
What did Mary see?

Could she know that his hands would be pierced when he
died?
That the world would demand that he be crucified?
That he'd return from the grave to make men justified?
What did Mary see?

She saw in her hand God's miraculous joy.
Her child, Messiah, was also God's boy.
Sent to earth God's plan to deploy.
That's what Mary saw.

A tiny hand reached for Mary's that night and
depended completely on her.
That same hand still reaches for you and asks that you now
depend completely on him. Will you see all that Mary saw?

Luke 1:46-47

"And Mary said: 'My soul glorifies the Lord and my spirit
rejoices in God my Savior.'"

JOSEPH'S SON

God chose a simple carpenter
To raise his Son on earth.
He wasn't a king, or a wealthy man
Born of noble birth.

But a hardworking, honest man was he
With more faith than even he knew.
To trust that God would always provide
While in wisdom and stature Christ grew.

Now while Joseph knew that this was the Christ,
He treated him just like his own
And gave him the love that only he could
And protected him till he was grown.

He taught him his trade, to work with his hands.
He taught him whatever he could.
He prepared him for all that God had in store
The same way all good fathers would.

Imagine the smiles that came his way
While raising God's only pure Son.
Imagine the fears and the dreams as well
In making sure that the task got done.

We tend to forget what all he gave up
To raise this child, the Christ.
We tend to forget the obedience he had
And also what he sacrificed.

Love for his God and then for his Son
Gave strength to do what was needed.
The end of his life is not even known
But I'm sure at Christ's feet Joseph's seated.

Matthew 1:24-25

"When Joseph woke up, he did what the angel of the Lord had commanded him and took Mary home as his wife. But he had no union with her until she gave birth to a son. And he gave him the name Jesus."

A CHRISTMAS RESPONSE

"Hugs and kisses to the birthday boy!"
My seven year old exclaims.
"Tomorrow is Christmas day, oh joy!"
Her love for Jesus proclaims.

"I love you, Jesus," the next one cries
In the middle of her prayers.
Do you suppose an angel sighs
To know that children care?

"Thank you for dying on the cross,"
My oldest says to God.
She knows our lives are not a loss
And gives him glory and laud.

What do you say at Christmas time?
Do you come to celebrate
With faith like a child filled with joy at the plan
That our Father chose to create?

Psalm 8:2a

"From the lips of children and infants
 you have ordained praise."

WISE MEN STILL SEEK HIM

Consider the Magi with worldly fame,
Seeking a baby, they knew not his name,
But they knew he was special, he was to be King.
So to him gifts of value, special gifts did they bring.

And what did they do when they saw the wee lad?
They bowed down in worship and gave what they had.
After months of searching for the small baby boy,
God rewarded them fully and gave them great joy.

They went back home with lives totally changed.
That happened the way that God had arranged.
For you see, if you seek him with all of your heart,
You're promised that in your life he'll be part.

So be like the wise men seeking to find
The one who'll take everything hurtful and bind
It instead into new life filled with joy.
It's your blessing for seeking that one little boy.

Jeremiah 29:13

"You will seek me and find me when you seek me with all
your heart."

IMAGININGS

Imagine yourself on a night long ago
As a shepherd whose sheep graze in soft moonlit glow.
With your rod and your staff lying closely nearby
While you're singing a little lamb's soft lullaby.

Imagine yourself, if you will, lying still
Beneath a night canopy of stars on your hill.
With the sweet gentle sound of the bleating of sheep
Comforting you as you drift off to sleep.

Imagine amazement you'd feel when you'd hear,
The voices of angels ring in your ears.
They brought forth the news of a Savior's new birth.
In the small town of David, lay hope for the earth.

Imagine the worship that you would have felt
As you came before Jesus and then humbly knelt
By the manger that held what the angels declared.
Through this tiny small being your life could be spared.

Imagine the joy that would come to your heart
When you realized God had picked you for a part
In bringing the news to each person that night
To share what you learned from that glorious sight.

Imagine, imagine we still feel today
The joy in our hearts that comes when we pray.
Christ Jesus was born to both shepherds and kings
To bring life full of joy and all perfect things.

Luke 2:15,17

"When the angels had left them and gone into heaven, the shepherds said to one another, 'Let's go to Bethlehem and see this thing that has happened, which the Lord has told us about.' When they had seen him, they spread the word concerning what had been told them about this child."

CHRISTMAS LOVE

A heart that's overflowing and filled with peace and love,
A confidence in knowing the Savior from above,
A warming of the heart, a swelling of great joy,
Came to us one Christmas morn through God's small baby
boy.

Millions come to know him, to trust his saving grace
And let him fill their every need and every empty place.
For Christ, God's Son, the Savior, can take an empty heart
And fill to overflowing every drained and hollow part.

Your heart, your soul, and your mind can be completely filled
When you come before the Savior and let your heart be stilled.
Listen to the words, and feel the gentle touch
Of Jesus Christ, the Savior, who loves you, oh so much.

When Christmas morning comes and you rise to greet the day
Feel the love that Jesus holds that never fades away.
May your heart be filled with laughter that only Jesus gives.
May you know the love there is for you because the Savior
lives.

Romans 5:5

"And hope does not disappoint us, because God has poured
out his love into our hearts by the Holy Spirit, whom he has
given us."

IF WE ONLY BELIEVE

A virgin gave birth to God's Son long ago,
If we only believe.
He lay in the manger so humble and low,
If we only believe.

He grew tall in stature and in love for his God,
If we only believe.
For peace we can come to his staff and his rod,
If we only believe.

He could offer not riches, but something much more,
If we only believe.
His death on the cross opens wide heaven's door,
If we only believe.

He forgives us our sins; his love we can't sever,
If we only believe.
Eternal new life can be ours now and forever,
If we only believe.

John 20:31

"But these things are written that you may believe that Jesus is the Christ, the Son of God, and that by believing you may have life in his name."

ONE TINY BABY

On a lonely, dark hillside, one night long ago,
Fast asleep in a manger in the moonlight's soft glow
Lay a small, tiny baby who'd bring peace to mankind.
He'd give love and sweet healing, bring sight to the blind.

As Mary and Joseph gazed in awe at his face
They knew this was God's gift no one could replace.
The true gift of love came to earth on that night,
For God had diminished our darkness with light.

A wee, little baby who would give us his all,
How could so much love come from someone so small?
Yet God in his wisdom set in action his plan.
His love to the world sent through two tiny hands.

It was one tiny baby giving love and true peace.
Through that one, tiny baby we find our release.
For the Father in heaven gave his only dear Son.
Through that one tiny baby our new life has begun.

Luke 2:11-12

"Today in the town of David a Savior has been born to you;
he is Christ the Lord. This will be a sign to you: You will find
a baby wrapped in cloths and lying in a manger."

A Cold Heart

A man's cold heart is a sad condition
In need of an agent of change.
His heart is full of an unspoken rendition
Of meaningless lyrics so strange.
A cold weary heart has to strain every day
Just to keep up with the pace
Of an unattached world that seems willing to say
For you I haven't a place.
But long, long ago a baby was born
Who also had no place to stay.
On a cold Christmas eve in a stable so worn
The Savior was laid in the hay.
That is the reason a cold heart can be lined
And warmed by God's infinite grace.
Because of his birth each heart then can find
Next to Jesus a warm special place.

Matthew 24:12-13

"Because of the increase of wickedness, the love of most will grow cold, but he who stands firm to the end will be saved."

THE VIGIL OF THE TREE

Plain and unadorned on a quiet lonely hill,
The tree stood tall and vigilant in the darkness, oh so still.
No rustling of the boughs, or stirring deep within,
The tree looked on in wonder at a baby's childish grin.
The angel choir now silent, the shepherds gone away,
But the tree still kept on watching until darkness turned to day.
The tree had no conception, no understanding mind.
No grasp of what the tiny babe would mean to all mankind.
The years went by, the tree grew old, his life was almost done.
But his heart could still remember clearly Mary and Joseph's
    son.
Savior, now they called him. Whatever did that mean?
What happened to the little child born in the manger scene?
Could it be that God had sent a Savior to the earth?
Could it be the tree had witnessed a Savior's holy birth?
Conversation changed, discontented folks walked by,
And the tree heard they had sentenced God's Savior to die.
This cannot be, I will hold a vigil for his cause.
He cannot die; the Savior has not broken any laws.
The stubborn tree determined to stand at any cost,
Then angry men cut him down; it seemed that all was lost.
Into a cross they made the tree to be carried up a hill
To hold the gentle Savior and carry out God's will.
Somehow it seemed so fitting for the tree to be the one
That held the final vigil of holding up God's Son.
For deep within the tree, he knew this was not all,
That God would raise the Savior who would give salvation's
    call.

The vigil of the tree from the starry, moonlit night
Ended with a promise of God's Son; the gift of light.
From Christmas time to Easter, there is no greater love
Than Jesus Christ, the Savior, sent to us from God above.

1 Peter 2:24

"He himself bore our sins in his body on the tree, so that we might die to sins and live for righteousness; by his wounds you have been healed."

GOD'S CHILD

He came as a child to make us his children.
He came as a babe to show love.
He came into our world without celebration.
He came with God's peace from above.

He grew as a child grows in stature and wisdom.
He grew and his faith became strong.
He grew and he taught what the Father had taught him.
He grew and he never did wrong.

He lived as a child lives, so simple and humble.
He lived facing all that we face.
He lived with emotions meant only for humans.
He lived all our hurts to erase.

He loved as a child loves, without hesitation.
He loved with his heart, soul, and mind.
He loved without fear of the hurt it would cause him.
He loved wholly to die for mankind.

Matthew 18:4

"Therefore, whoever humbles himself like this child is the greatest in the kingdom of heaven."

THE TRUE MIRACLE

When Jesus was born on that night long ago,
A small tiny babe with his eyes all aglow,
Some said, "It's a miracle sent from above!
A miracle, a sign of God's awesome love!"
The heavenly angel choir calling his name,
The lowing of sheep acknowledged he came,
The wise men, the star, and all other signs
Were not the focus of God's miraculous design.
A true miracle brings a change of the heart.
A true miracle brings a changed life and new start.
Yes, God's miracle came that night through his Son
When the work that he did on this earth was all done.
You ask what the true miracle ever could be?
The miracle, in truth, is he loves you and me.
Our Father in heaven sent his dear Son to die
That we could have life everlasting on high.
And miracle of miracles, Jesus said, "Yes!"
And those who will love him forever are blessed.
So at Christmas this year, please remember as you
Celebrate joyously all the things that you do,
The true miracle's message that Christmas can bring
Is that Jesus, the Babe, is your Savior and King.

Hebrews 1:3

"The Son is the radiance of God's glory and the exact representation of his being, sustaining all things by his powerful word. After he had provided purification for sins, he sat down at the right hand of the Majesty in heaven."

THE PALM OF HIS HAND

I asked God one day to give me a sign
That proved his love and his grace.
I didn't need much—an encouraging word
To fill my heart's empty place.

"I want you to know that I never forget
Any part of your life," he said.
"So listen closely and hear what I say.
Let your heart by my words be led.

When I sent my Son on that night long ago,
It fulfilled a great part of my plan.
For I've never forgotten my love for you;
You're engraved on the palm of my hand.

You see, Jesus was born to live and to die
So you'd know my love and my grace.
I love you so much that I gave him away
To live and then die in your place.

Engraved on my palm and now on his too,
That was pierced because of our love.
The sign that you want came the first Christmas night
When my Son came from heaven above."

Isaiah 49:16a

"See I have engraved you on the palms of my hands."

THE SHOUTS OF THE ANGELS

The shouts of the angels filled all the earth
Proclaiming their joy in the wonderful birth.
Angels rejoiced in the knowledge that when
Men of all nations learned to depend
On this great gift of God given in grace,
Then hearts would be changed and sorrow displaced.
Salvation is given through Jesus the Christ.
The angels knew triumph when they spoke that night.
"Don't be afraid. I bring you good news.
Your Savior is born if only you'll choose
To love him and give him the whole of your heart.
Your peace is in him. Today's a new start.
God's blessings to you, every man, woman, and child,
Is found in this babe born so meek and so mild.
But don't be deceived by what you see here.
This babe has the power to chase away fear.
No longer do you have to face life alone.
God sent you this blessing from his holy throne.
Open your eyes to the gift you've received
On this one holy night. Rejoice and believe!"
The angel's message speaks to us today.
Will we believe in the Savior or send him away?

Psalm 66: 1-2

"Shout with joy to God, all the earth!
    Sing the glory of his name;
    make his praise glorious!"

NEW YEAR'S FIRST SNOW

New Year's first snow lies fresh on the ground.
New winter beauty in silence abounds.
It's fresh and it's new with a crispness of season.
Children's smiles on sleds; God gave snow for this reason.
Every change that we see as God creates a new day
Can bring fresh contentment for a child at play.
If I can find joy as my life flies by,
Then I can find peace and realize why
It's only through God I'll find contentment this year
As I pray every day and ask God to draw near.

Proverbs 19:23

"The fear of the Lord leads to life:
    Then one rests content, untouched by trouble."

WEEP NOT FOR ME

Dry your tears; weep not for me.
I'm in joyous splendor and finally free
Of all pain and suffering I felt in my life.
Weep not for me; I'm free from all strife.

Weep not for me, I've finally found
Peace and contentment, I rejoice at the sound
Of heaven's full chorus singing wondrous refrains.
Weep not for me; I've forgotten the pain.

Weep not for me, but for those that I love.
I'm waiting to join with them here up above.
Please fill their needs until we meet again
Never let them forget the victory we win.

I know that someday we'll be face to face;
I can't wait till we meet in this glorious place.
It's better than ever I thought it could be,
When I got here and my Savior did see.

So please dry your tears; find the joy that's still there.
Remember the great times that we got to share.
But know there'll be more times in heaven some day.
So weep not for me, for I've come home to stay.

Isaiah 25:8

"He will swallow up death forever.
The sovereign Lord will wipe away the tears
    from all faces;
he will remove the disgrace of his people
    from all the earth.
The Lord has spoken."

AT HIS FEET

In my mind I picture Jesus
With me sitting at his feet
Looking into eyes where compassion
And love in one look finally meet.

I lay my head against his knee.
He gently strokes my hair.
I'll never feel more loved and cared for
Than when I worship him there.

I know he has millions of loved ones,
I know that he loves them all.
Yet he's never forgotten or left me
When I on his name had to call.

No matter what pain that I go through,
No matter how badly I feel,
His peace and his comfort are constant.
His love and protection are real.

My favorite time to be with him
Is when I look into his face.
I've found joy and lasting contentment
At his feet when my problems I place.

So I'll rely on Jesus, my Savior,
To uphold me when I cannot walk.
He's my shepherd. I know that he loves me.
I've a special place in his flock.

Psalm 9:9-10

"The Lord is a refuge for the oppressed,
    a stronghold in times of trouble.
Those who know your name will trust in you,
    for you, Lord, have never forsaken those who seek you."

THE POTTER'S CLAY

My soul is just a lump of clay
Held in the Potter's hand.
He looks at it and then begins
To mold me by his plan.

Before I let him mold me
Creating something new,
I really had to struggle
My life each day construe.

But now it is so easy
To let him do the work
Of molding and perfecting,
Removing tainted quirks.

I never have to worry
About how I'll turn out,
Because the Master Potter
Has removed all of my doubt.

He tells me he can do it all
And in the end I'll see
The beauty that the Potter
Has created within me.

Jeremiah 18:6

"'O house of Israel, can I not do with you as this potter
does?' declares the Lord. 'Like clay in the hand of the potter,
so are you in my hand, O house of Israel.'"

My Future Hope

Where is hope when hope seems lost?
My hope is in the Lord.
It is through him and no one else
I've found my faith restored.

I cannot trust my earthly self
To bring me joy and peace.
It's only through my hope in God
I find my sweet release.

This earth will never fill me up
With what I really need.
It's heaven where I'll be content,
My hope fulfilled indeed.

So though my body soon must die,
My hope shall never leave.
I live by faith and not by sight.
My soul he will receive.

And for those I leave behind
Please know I yearn for this:
That on the day of hope restored
We'll share in heaven's bliss.

2 Corinthians 5:6-8

"Therefore we are always confident and know that as long as we are at home in the body we are away from the Lord. We live by faith, not by sight. We are confident, I say, and would prefer to be away from the body and at home with the Lord."

THE RACE AHEAD

I have fully determined to run the race ahead
And focus on my Jesus and go where he has led.

I know it won't be easy to be what I should be.
Yet at the end he's promised his appearing I will see.

The race will take much training and at times I'll lose my
    way,
But I'll focus on my Jesus to lead me day by day.

And when I feel so tired, like my strength is almost gone,
I'll focus on my Jesus and find strength to carry on.

When the race is almost over, and the finish line's in sight,
I'll soar towards the finish as though a bird in flight.

And when the race is finished and I'm in heaven's land
I will with my dear Savior walk forever hand in hand.

2 Timothy 4:7-8

"I have fought the good fight, I have finished the race, I
have kept the faith. Now there is in store for me the crown
of righteousness, which the Lord, the righteous Judge, will
award to me on that day—and not only to me, but also to
all who have longed for his appearing."

TO SEARCH THE HEAVENS

As the lily unfolds her petals, straining to touch the sky,
So I search the heavens above me waiting for the time to fly.

I look forward with joy to that moment when God comes to
    take me away.
I'll worship him in his presence, by his side forever I'll stay.

It will happen in only a twinkle, in just the blink of an eye
That I'll be in the presence of Jesus, and find peace by and by.

Now I might fly in an airplane, or even a hot air balloon,
But it's not like flying with Jesus. That day just can't come
    too soon.

To leave the cares of this world to find perfect life evermore.
I'll never need worry my heart again for I shall cry no more.

Yet, I fear for those left behind here who haven't felt his touch,
And I pray that each one will find him, the one they need
    so much.

So as I strain my eyes toward heaven searching to see his face,
May I be his light to all I see and help them, too, win the race.

1 Corinthians 15:51-52

"Listen, I tell you a mystery: We will not all sleep, but we will
all be changed—in a flash, in the twinkling of an eye, a the
last trumpet. For the trumpet will sound, the dead will be
raised imperishable, and we will be changed."

A Believer's Song

Death can be a friend for those who faithfully believe
That Jesus Christ has died for them; their souls he will
    receive.

It's hard for friends and family who all are left behind,
But Jesus can reunite them all in his own given time.

Now it's just a separation from earth to heaven above.
We're all one in his Spirit and in his precious love.

May strength and power come to you from his almighty hand
Until we're all together in the perfect, promised land.

Have faith in God's tomorrows. He'll always see you through.
He'll carry you on journeys far past death to make you new.

1 Corinthians 15:54-55

"When the perishable has been clothed with the imperishable, and the mortal with immortality, then the saying that is written will come true; 'Death has been swallowed up in victory.'

> 'Where, O death, is your victory?
> Where, O death, is your sting?'"

WE SHALL BE LIKE JESUS

We shall be like Jesus, clothed in linen white.
Our sinful self destroyed, our soul made wholly right.
And the promise that he gives, is pain will be no more
On the day that we'll be like him and enter heaven's door.

We shall be like Jesus. Full of joy within his arms.
All evil left behind us nevermore to see earth's harms.
And the promise that we feel here is peace in Jesus' name.
I can't wait to be like him, free of all my guilt and shame.

We shall be like Jesus on the day that he appears
In his glorious sovereign splendor, he'll draw his loved ones
near.
He'll take his children homeward in joy and tranquil
peace.
To be like him will bring me blessed, sweet release.

We shall be like Jesus, what a fight of grace God gave
When he sent his Son to heal us, forgive us, and to save.
Lord, help me to be like Jesus now as I go through my day.
Mold your divine ideal into my simple lump of clay.

1 John 3:2

"Dear friends, now we are children of God, and what we
will be has not yet been made known. But we know that
when he appears, we shall be like him, for we shall see him
as he is."

A NEW DAY

There will come a day I know
When rivers of peace will always flow.
And wolf and lamb together lie
In that new day when death will die.

God promises eternal life,
A life that's free from pain and strife.
It is a gift to those who love
The God who reigns in heaven above.

Can you seek eternal things
And claim the promises they bring?
Believe in him and in his word
The sweetest promises ever heard.

While things of earth can bring you down
And replace your joy with saddened frown,
Place your focus upon your Lord
Where all your promises are stored.

Remember you have been released
And one day suffering will cease.
Until that day when all is new
Cling to Christ and his promises too.

Isaiah 11:6

"The wolf will live with the lamb,
    the leopard will lie down with the goat,
the calf and the lion and the yearling together;
    and a little child will lead them."

GLORIOUS OBEDIENCE OF THE SON

Jesus brought his Father glory on our earth so long ago,
That God would give back glory and then the earth would
    know
The only true and perfect man who came to earth to save.
Jesus was the Son of God. His perfect life he gave.

He finished every tiny task that God gave him to do.
He never grumbled; simply did what God had asked him to.
And now in glory Jesus rules beside his Father's throne.
And at the end of earthly life he calls the faithful home.

For God has promised glorious life to all who will obey.
That began with his dear Son and continues on today.
The challenge, then, is in my life to glorify him, too.
May everything I do today, Lord, show my love for you.

For life has been a challenge, Lord, to live as you desire,
That you would turn me into gold and refine me with life's
    fire.
And when I'm in your presence with my work completely
    done,
May you give me glory, too, the way you did your Son.

John 17:4-5

"I have brought you glory on earth by completing the work
you gave me to do. And now, Father, glorify me in your presence with the glory I had with you before the world began."

BEYOND THE SUNRISE

Take me past the sunrise into that other land
That I might glimpse the heavens and hold my Savior's hand.
Take me past the sunrise to the glorious distant shore
Where peace and joy await me and I shall cry no more.

There is a promise waiting there, I found it in his word.
It's there beyond the sunrise I know his voice is heard.
Someday beyond the sunrise my life will be complete,
When I see the face of Jesus and kneel down at his feet.

How far beyond the sunrise do I really have to go
To feel his touch and healing, eternity to know?
I know it's something special that I just can't describe
It's there beyond the sunrise I'll be at Jesus' side.

I know beyond the sunrise all things will be the best,
And I will know contentment and perfect peace and rest.
Lord, help me see the sunrise in everything I do
Until the day you've promised my life you will renew.

Till then help me be patient with life upon this earth.
I know beyond the sunrise I'll find my perfect worth.
But here I must continue to do the things you say
And I'll fly beyond the sunrise on my appointed day.

Habakkuk 3:4

"His splendor was like the sunrise;
    rays flashed from his hand,
    where his power was hidden."

PW

To order additional copies of this title call:
1-877-421-READ (7323)
or please visit our Web site at
www.pleasantwordbooks.com

If you enjoyed this quality custom-published book,
drop by our Web site for more books and information.

www.winepressgroup.com
"Your partner in custom publishing."

Printed in the United States
220036BV00001B/6/P

9 781414 112640